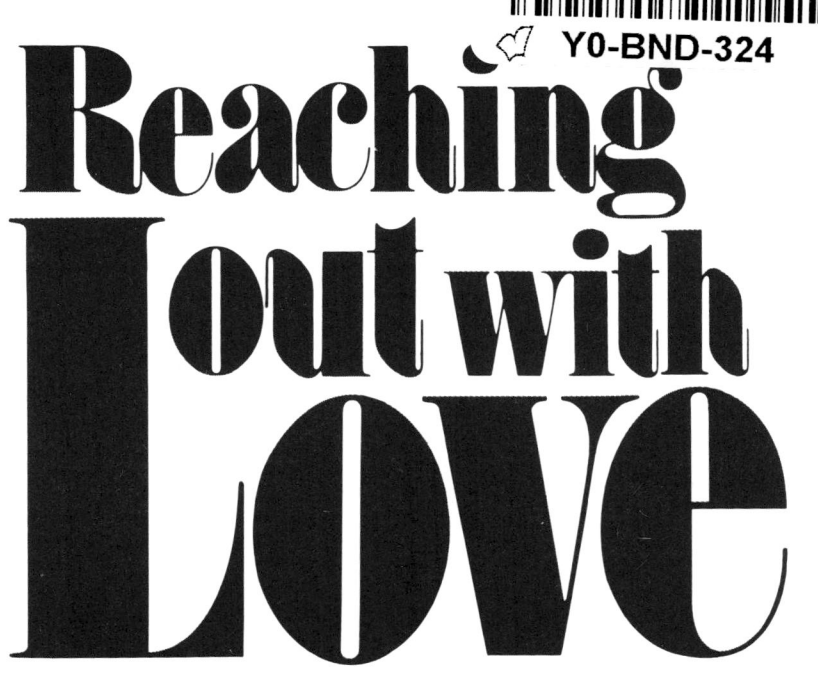

Reaching out with Love

Encounters with troubled youth

by Jean Marie Campbell

foreword by Ann Kiemel

STANDARD PUBLISHING
Cincinnati, Ohio   3652

In order to give anonymity to the individuals portrayed in this book, all names have been changed, as well as the minor facts and sequence of events. The conflicts and insights brought about by each encounter, however, are accurately recorded.

Scripture quotations are from The New American Standard Bible, © The Lockman Foundation 1960, 1962, 1963, 1968, 1971, 1972, 1973, 1975, and are used by permission.

Library of Congress Cataloging in Publication Data

Campbell, Jean Marie.
  Reaching out with love.

  1. Problem children—Education. I. Title.
LC4801.C34   371.93   81-50354
ISBN 0-87239-453-0 (pbk.)   AACR2

© 1981, The STANDARD PUBLISHING Company, Cincinnati, Ohio.
  A Division of STANDEX INTERNATIONAL Corporation.
  Printed in U.S.A.

For
Two Teachers

Ruth Ann Raymond
and
Marjorie Dymale

Foreword

this book
is about a lady
who loved kids.
who traced their hurts
and struggles
and failures
and placed stretches of sunrise
across their lives.
it is a book
about a public school,
and a teacher
who took Jesus
there.
it is beautiful
and gentle.
it is one woman
plus God
plus love
in her corner
of the world.

                                        ann kiemel
                                        boston
                                        1980

Preface

I hated school. The confinement. The tug of war with studies. The seemingly endless journey of twelve l-o-n-g years. Yet when it came to choosing a career, I gravitated back to the only life I'd really known—the classroom—and decided to approach school one more time from an entirely different perspective. This time I would be in charge. This time I would hold the reins.

In college, however, something dramatic and unexpected happened in my life: *I became a Christian.* Not a middle of the road, nominal, ho-hum professor of Christ, but one who had unequivocally committed all her strengths and talents to be used for her king and in His kingdom. This offering of myself back to God quite naturally included my desire to teach.

Over the years I could never understand those Christian educators who shamefully buried their faith in the sand when it came to their influence in the public schools. Nor could I comprehend the motivations of overly zealous Christians who literally battled to indoctrinate, to push, to shove their faith into the foreground. It was early in my career, during those first months on my own, that I realized I needed to strike a healthy balance between the two extremes.

Surprisingly, I found very little printed matter available to guide me in my struggles. No one to identify with. No one who could spell out the dangers, sacrifices, excitement, and victories. And finally, after ignoring the obvious for several years and the constant prompting of a dear friend, the message came through: perhaps it was my task to write the book I had wanted and needed to read.

There are three brief experiences I'd like to share which shaped my attitudes and approaches in education. The first of these has to do with my own salvation. I don't think it was by accident that it was a teacher who led me to Christ. I think it was a deliberate act of God to continually remind me that teachers *can* reach. It had happened to me!

Secondly, I received a revelation during my first job interview. I'll never forget the many questions I had to answer from a standardized booklet, the tape recorder which documented each word I said, and my own uneasiness at this new "first." Of all the questions that afternoon, one stood out and totally baffled me. "Think back to your student teaching encounter," my interviewer said. "What problem in education bothers you the most as you reflect?"

For two awkward, silent minutes I watched the tape reels turn round and round, and then I answered. "I guess what bothers me the most is my long-range effectiveness as a teacher. It has just now occurred to me that some of the students I left last week will be dead in ten years. Some will have lost children. Perhaps arms or legs. A few even the will to live. Others will be divorced. I have to ask myself what I can do to prepare them for real-life crises ahead. Can I prepare them? As good as our school systems are, could it be that we've failed in the greatest task of all? The task of teaching kids how to live? That's what bothers me. How can I make a difference?"

Those words have hung in the back of my mind ever since and pricked my conscience into outward action.

A third experience which helped to focus my goals in education came at the end of my first year as a freshman English teacher. There was a period of time when I toyed with the idea of leaving the classroom for a degree in guidance counseling. There, I figured, I would have many more opportunities to touch the lives of searching students.

I made an important discovery during my consultation with half a dozen guidance counselors from different area schools. They all agreed that more counseling went on between teachers and students in the classrooms than ever occurred in guidance offices. If this was true, then I concluded that my place of greatest effectiveness was right back in my original career choice—the classroom.

May I add one final note? Although the arena in which my stories take place is the public school system, there are obvious lessons which can be applied to all walks of life. Each of us, whoever we are and whatever we do, has a mission field here and now for which we are truly accountable. Our eagerness to be used is all God needs to begin a special work in us and through us.

My years of experience are not many, both as a Christian and as a teacher, and there are failures for every successful story here. Bear with me. I am still growing. I am still changing. And I am open to learn new things from you.

June 1981

The Primer Lesson

Jesus,
here i am.
i have a slip of paper today which
guarantees my skill as a teacher.
me
who hated school *so* much.
me
unpolished, inexperienced, unsophisticated.
me
young voyager in life and scared.
Jesus,
You never had degrees or a piece of paper
and You were a teacher
first class.
You cared.
You reached.
You made the lowliest of life feel
significance and inestimable worth.
You led the way.

Rabboni,
You said it was enough for the disciple
to be as his teacher.
imagine me
trying to fill Your shoes.
imagine me
Your representative on earth.
and yet here i am (paper and all)
with a couple hundred students who
call me teacher.
Rabboni,
make me fitting to bear Your name.
use this classroom
to care.
to reach.
to make the lowliest of life feel
significance and inestimable worth.
only lead the way:
teach me.

1

Monica, Monica, Why Do You Hate Me?

Whoever said a teacher's job is easy, obviously has never taught. Whether in the public or private sector, whether in the suburb or inner city, teaching's hard business. It really is.

No matter how much college training a person may have in preparation for a career in education, the old saying is still true: there is no teacher like experience. And, I might add, there is no experience for a teacher quite like that first year. Any remaining illusions about education and the idealistic "save the world" notions will inevitably be tried and retried when a teacher-in-the-making steps from textbook theory to actual real-life practice.

My first year adventures in the public schools were not unusually different from what was to be expected. Like others who suddenly found themselves in their own classrooms for the first time, I faced my share of new and exhausting adjustments. It was difficult enough to learn how and what to teach for my six freshman English classes, but I also had the added pressures of advising the school's yearbook, co-directing the spring drama, and coping with the politics of administrative personnel. Yet with due respect to the whirlwind of demands, I still maintain the biggest problem that first year came in the form of a fifteen-year-old girl named Monica Thomas. Somehow any other struggle looked minor when compared to the dilemmas I faced with her.

If I cried that first year (and I did!), it was over Monica. If I allowed myself to get angry and discouraged, it had to do with Monica. If I spent more time in early morning prayer, it was because I needed extra strength to face Monica. And if I wanted to quit teaching *forever,* it stemmed from my fear that hundreds of Monicas were eagerly waiting in the world for a similar test of wills.

How well I remember the first time we met on the opening day of school. Opening days always breed confusion, but adding to the normal stress one such as Monica made mine unforgettable. It was late afternoon and my sixth class had just begun. About thirty students had lined up along the back of the room, and as I called their names they were seated alphabetically.

When this was done, I introduced myself and shared a brief overview of English I. "We'll talk more about classwork in a few minutes. First, I need some general facts from you," I said. "I'm passing out information and activity cards which need to be completed. Don't write on them yet until I explain the order of questions." I was handing out cards to the final row of students when suddenly the classroom door slammed shut. Startled, all heads turned toward the distraction.

Before I had a chance to speak, a few students groaned jokingly, "Oh, no! Not Thomas! Thomas isn't in here, is she?" Surprise and excitement were conveyed in their voices. Thomas, apparently, was the smiling tall girl who leaned against the door.

"Looks that way. Better get used to it!" she announced, flipping her long brunette hair over her shoulder. Students replied in a chorus of "Oh, no," "not in here?" and "tell us you're joking!"

"Excuse me," I interrupted as I reached for the computer listing on my desk. "What's your name?"

She did not answer. Many of her friends burst out in laughter.

"Do you belong in 310? What's your name?" I repeated.

"Oh," she smiled and said slowly with a phony southern accent, "are y'all talkin' to little ol' me?"

"Yes I'm—"

She put one hand up to the side of her face, blinked wildly and addressed the class, "Chillins, is she talkin' to little ol' me?"

Everybody was amused at her dramatic entrance except me.

"Young lady, I *am* talking to you and I need to know where you belong. This is the first day of school, you're over ten minutes late, and I don't have a Thomas on my class roster."

"You're new here, aren't you?" she asked sarcastically. "I just bet you are." The tone in her voice and the way she rolled her eyes upward made everyone stop laughing. Someone across the room whispered, "Way to go, Thomas! On the first day of school!"

I did not dare look away from Monica, nor did I dare reinforce to anyone my newness. After a few seconds I walked toward her, held out my hand and said, "Your schedule sheet?"

"See for yourself, Warden," she said and reached into the top center pocket of her bib overalls. "If it's any of your business, Mr. Campton just now changed it. I was scheduled for junior English. Hey—imagine me in junior English!" Some students chuckled, but not many.

The assistant principal had indeed made a notation on her sheet. He wrote in the margin, "Computer error. Rescheduled to 310—Campbell."

"Fine," I acknowledged, "have a seat back there and I'll add your name to my list."

"Have a seat?" she mocked. "Well, now. You're mighty generous with school property!"

"I'm sure you know what I mean. Here's your schedule sheet."

She snatched it from my hand. "And remember, Honey," she added while turning from me toward the back of the room, "Monica Thomas knows where she's supposed to be and what she wants. Got that?"

"And *you* remember that my name is Miss Campbell and I'm the one in charge here," I answered, hoping my voice sounded convincingly forceful.

She didn't respond aloud to the class this time. Instead she grumbled, "Sure, sure. We'll just see," under her breath. Monica threw her notebook on a back desk and plopped herself into a seat along the wall of plate glass windows.

What a relief! Everything was quiet again, so I resumed my instructions on the activity cards. "That should pretty much do it," I said, "but just in case—" I was cut off.

"I ain't got no card," Monica blurted out louder than I.

In the confusion I had forgotten to make sure she had one. I walked over to hand an extra card to a student in her row and stated, "By the way, if any of you have comments or questions, the rule is you raise your hand first and wait to be addressed properly. Now—"

"All I said was, I ain't got one," she reiterated.

"I understand what you've said, Monica." My voice grew strong, "But perhaps you've missed my point. Raise your hand in the future."

"I only meant—"

"Save it," I said and continued. "Last of all, print carefully on your cards because the lines are narrow. You can begin."

I was absolutely terrified when I saw Monica's hand shoot up. At least, I reasoned, she had followed directions this time. "Yes, Monica, what is it?"

"What if I don't want to print, Miss Teacher Lady?"

"My name is Miss Campbell."

"What if I don't want to print, Miss Teacher Lady?"

How do I handle this one? I was trembling inside. "Then write neatly."

She smiled wide and responded, "What if I don't know how?"

"Then do the best you can!"

"Are you sure you can handle my best, Honey? You certainly don't *look* like it!"

"I can handle all sorts of things," I said. "Now back to your card."

I thought I had heard the last of her until I noticed her hand in the air. "Monica?"

"Why do you need to know all this stuff anyway? I'm taking mine home. That is, if I decide to do it. It's hard!" She deliberately talked like someone half her age. Class members were trying to keep their composure. A few were shaking their heads back and forth in disbelief.

"If you're having trouble with your name, address, or *whatever*, then maybe you'd better see me after class. Everyone, get busy with your cards," I stated.

Fortunately that was the last of the debating for our first time together. It was enough of a foretaste, however, to unnerve me the rest of the day and evening. Why did I feel so threatened by Monica? Was I overreacting? Was I inviting her to continue? Would she always be challenging and bold?

"Father," I prayed, "I can't sleep tonight because I'm too wide-awake and afraid. So much has happened today and everything—absolutely everything—is new. Close to 200 kids passed through my room today and their names and faces and classes all blur together. Some looked friendly, some afraid, and some rough. But do you know who scares me the most? The only face and name I can remember—Monica Thomas. How do I begin to handle her? I feel like I'm falling apart when she talks to me in that swaggering tone of voice. Father, help me make it through tonight. Help me go back tomorrow. Keep me in one piece."

It was a miracle but I made it through another day and then the next. My first priority was to establish discipline in each of my classes. Some groups settled in well and were easy to harness, yet Monica's class baffled me more than all the others combined. The testing and tug-of-war between Monica and me continued from day-to-day. Her questions and remarks about every rule, every assignment, every piece of classroom conversation were becoming a constant source of irritation to me. The disputes increased in number and strength as weeks passed by, and I was convinced that her efforts held the entire group back.

Other teachers who had Monica in class were sympathetic and supportive to me in ways I needed, but they also had several more years of conditioning from which to draw strength. "Jean," they reminded me, "Thomas is prone to be aggressive and demanding on even her best days. Keep trying, you're bound to find the best approach to handle things your way. You'll make it." Nothing short of trial and error, victories and defeats would teach me how to muscle my own authority and mean it through words and gestures. I had to learn those lessons on my own and at my own pace.

On one hand I wanted to instill the fear of God in Monica, and on the other I wanted to win her over quietly. It was my pride which kept me from sending her to the office even when I was sure she deserved to go. I guess I didn't want to admit she was beyond me. There were also the frequent warnings about the office's lack of stern discipline which made me wary. "Even if you use the office as your last resort," the teachers in the lounge cautioned, "that's no assurance you'll get results. They'll send her right back to you. Count on it. They'd rather believe we have hang-ups, not the kids. So you're better off to handle her yourself."

I decided it was time to experiment with some of the techniques I'd learned in student teaching. I tried ignoring Monica, I tried moving her seat, I tried giving her positive attention about her dress or appearance. I tried forceful words when she got sassy (was she any other way?), and I tried pleasant smiles. I tried talking with her alone and I tried sitting down with her in the guidance office. I got nowhere. She refused to say anything to me personally or to the counselor except that she hated my class and she hated me. What a simple remark to come from such a complex relationship.

It's an understatement to say something had to be done for the sake of my class and me. I was putting too much time and worry into one isolated student. I was miserable! Finally I had a long talk with Mr. Campton, the assistant principal. "She won't listen to me, Bill, and her class is more like a circus at times. She'll generally stop talking when I reach the angry stage, then she plays little mumble, 'catch me if you can' games to get in the last word. I've tried all the psychological angles I know to try, but nothing's worked permanently. She'll back away for a few minutes or even a whole class period, yet the silence never lasts. Where do I draw the line, and how much do I take?"

He was a quiet and calming man, not at all like the stereotyped rough-and-ready principals I'd known while growing up. "How do the students in the class react to her?" he asked.

"Monica is some kind of a leader to them. Some think she's the funniest act they've seen; they're also the ones failing the tests right along with her. A couple of the serious students are starting to resent the wasted time and stupid remarks. The majority of kids are in the middle. They smile when she interrupts, but they're too shy to say anything. I think they're afraid of getting on her wrong side, or even mine, for that matter."

"I've heard her name mentioned in here several times lately," he stated, "so I'll call her in. We'll see what good that does. In the meantime, why don't you get in touch with her parents and see what kind of cooperation they'll give?"

"Great," I said, "I'll gladly do it tonight. Be sure to let me know what happens on your end of things." For once I felt relaxed and on top of the situation.

It was seven o'clock when I decided to telephone Monica's parents. The phone rang and rang. "Yeah?" said a voice at the other end. It was Monica.

"Hello. May I speak to either Mr. or Mrs. Thomas?"

She paused. I was sure she recognized my voice. "Who's this?"

"Is your mother or father home? I'd like to speak to either of them."

"Who *is* this?"

Finally I admitted, "Monica, this is Miss Campbell. Can I speak with your mom or dad?"

There was an awkward moment of silence. "My mom's home, but she's busy. What do you want her for?"

"Is it possible you could get your mother? I'll wait. It'll only take a moment of her time," I said.

"I told you she was busy. *Now* what do you want?"

"When would be a good time to call back?" I was afraid she would hang up.

"I don't know. Not tonight! In fact, she's too busy to talk with you *anytime!*" Monica snapped.

Just then I overheard Mrs. Thomas in the background. She was arguing with Monica about the phone call. "I'll take it now. Who is it?"

"It's *dear* Miss Campbell from school. I told her you were busy but she won't tell me what she wants. It can't be important," Monica stated.

"Give me the phone," her mother replied.

"She's just going to tell you a pack of lies—"

"Monica, I want you to give me that phone," she demanded.

"Take it. I hope you and Miss Campbell have a good talk," she snarled. To my surprise she literally dropped the phone on the hardwood floor. Bang!

Her mother fumbled for the telephone and gave her final words to Monica, "Go to your room and don't listen in!"

"She's got to be kidding," I thought to myself, "Monica actually eavesdrops on her parents' conversations? What next?"

"Hello. I'm sorry to keep you waiting. This is Mrs. Thomas."

"Hi, I'm Miss Campbell and I have your daughter in my English class at school. I'm sorry for the inconvenience, but I'm calling because I need some advice. I was hoping you could help me."

"What's she done now?" her mother asked. She sounded extremely tired.

"I don't know how else to put it. Monica constantly talks back to me. She'll do anything to keep from cooperating, and she's failed each of the weekly tests. Frankly, I don't know how to settle her down or make her care about her grades. All I want is for her to come to class and stay quiet. That's all. Just stay quiet."

"Well, that sounds like Monica all right," her mother agreed.

There was silence for a few seconds. I continued, "What can you suggest? Call it a personality clash or whatever, I need help with her."

Just then we heard a click on the line and rock music in the background. "I figured this," Mrs. Thomas said, "she's picked up the other phone. I can tell." She sounded defeated. Almost hopeless.

Despite my personal amazement I had to continue, "Mrs. Thomas, what can you suggest?"

"All I can say is you do what you want. I don't know what's wrong with her. You don't have to say any more, I know what you're talking about because she acts that way here. She's run away from home three times and nothing we seem to do is right. Monica's our only child. You see, we couldn't have any more children after her. My husband . . . well . . . he's in and out of the hospital with leukemia. He's hardly ever at home and he's in no shape to make her behave."

She paused a long while then continued, this time a little more fortified, "I really don't know what to tell you. The last few years she's turned against everybody and I'm tired . . . I'm so tired of making excuses. She doesn't listen and she never has. I still have bruises from the last time she went on a rampage."

"I'm sorry about your husband," I said. "I had no idea."

"The strain here gets almost unbearable and it's all I can do to make it. You've got my permission to do whatever you want, but I don't think you'll ever break her know-it-all attitude. We haven't."

I thanked her for her understanding and wished her well. "I'll get back with you and let you know how she's doing for me," I said. Then the three of us hung up.

It was a long evening as I thought and prayed about the situation. My student Monica was now more than someone who sat in my room and disturbed me: she was a hurting individual who despised life. I acknowledged, that although I had started our relationship by hating the way she talked or acted, I had somehow begun to hate *her*. And there was a difference. Asking God for love to give Monica was hard because I still in part wanted to hang on to the grudges. After all, I considered, look at how upset I'd been at the end of so many days because of her taunting. Look at the times I had cried in frustration late at night, away from everyone. Look at her defiance!

"Father God," I sighed, "my attitude has soured over the past couple of months. I've wanted to wash my hands of Monica a hundred times over, and that's not right. I need Your help to walk back into class tomorrow and learn to cope with her. But could You do something more? I'm asking You to open a door for me to draw closer to her. To even win her over. To show her she has worth. I think that's what You want and I'm willing to try. Help me teach, Father, but more importantly, help me reach. I'd like to begin with Monica."

The following week was by far the best I'd experienced since school started. It was good because *my* attitude began to change the more I prayed for Monica. It was also good because Monica refused to talk to me or anyone else in class. Although her office visit may have triggered the angry silence, I suspected the real reason had to do with my call to her home. It was one thing for Monica to project the "I'm tough and my own boss" image to me earlier, but it was quite another thing now to be exposed as having lots of problems and being a problem herself. How it must have stung.

Our truce only lasted a week, yet it was a productive time for all of us. I enjoyed the inner peace of mind, her class was taught without distractions for a change, and Monica had time to cool down and think about her life. It all seemed so perfect. Unfortunately it didn't last long; another week passed and she returned to her former testy self. Prayers or no prayers, we were back to more struggles.

I want to mention one of the worst duties a teacher often had. It's what we called "pottie patrol" and, very simply, was the task of checking lavatories between classes for cigarette or pot smokers. None of us looked forward to this daily routine because it was about as non-academic as anything could be. Plus, it was an instant way to experience student hate if we caught and reported someone.

Since I was young and unfamiliar to most of the students at school, I had a rather good record of catching smoking offenders. It was tricky business, though, because it wasn't enough to smell smoke or see a blue cloud around a group of students. Suspension would only be enforced when a teacher literally saw a burning cigarette or joint in a student's hand.

One day in late November I stepped into the girls' rest room for a quick scan around the mirrors and fixtures. I smelled smoke and saw a circle of girls huddled along the far wall. (It was a typical smoking courtesy for a student to pass his or her cigarette from one friend to another.) I elbowed my way past twenty or so girls to the opposite corner of the room. That day I was unusually lucky because no one shouted "Teacher!" as a precaution to everyone else.

I moved quickly because each second counted. The girls were so busy puffing and passing they didn't see me push into their human chain until it was too late. I stood among them and watched Monica Thomas inhale and take the cigarette from her mouth. It was over, and she would face an automatic two-day suspension.

"Okay, ladies, back to class," I said. "Monica, I guess you get to come with me." I had reservations about the best course of action. If I took her to the office she would probably hate me forever. If I let her off the hook with a private warning I would either open the door of communication between us or, more likely, give her another opportunity to abuse my intentions.

"No matter what you think, Monica, I don't like having to turn you in. You know the rules on smoking and I'm sure you know about the consequences. Pick up your books and let's go," I said. Neither of us spoke another word as we walked to Bill Campton's office. She did not resist me physically or verbally, and I was proud of her for that.

Mr. Campton took us into his office right away. In a sentence or two I explained what had happened in the rest room. We both looked at Monica. "It's a lie, Mr. Campton, she's lying! She hates my guts and she only wants to get me out of her class!"

"Monica," I said while checking for Mr. Campton's response, "Monica, you know none of that is true. I was in the rest room. I saw you take the cigarette from your lips. I was there when you dropped it into the toilet. There were at least twenty others who saw you too."

"It ain't fair, Mr. Campton, she hates my guts!" Monica said with contempt. Then she began to cry.

Bill reached across his desk and offered her a tissue. "Were you or weren't you smoking?"

"All right I was. Is that what you want me to say? Yes, I was!" She continued to cry. "My mother is going to kill me when she finds out about this. And it's all your fault, Miss Campbell. It's all your fault."

I remained silent.

"Is someone at home now?" Mr. Campton asked.

"Just my mother," Monica sobbed, "only my mother." She blew her nose.

We remained in the office while Mr. Campton telephoned Mrs. Thomas. He explained the suspension rules to her and then listened quietly for a few moments. "Yes," he said, "I suppose we could do it that way, Mrs. Thomas. We don't have much need here for that, but I suppose we could try it in this case . . . okay . . . we'll get back to you. Good-by."

Both Monica and I waited to hear what course of action had been agreed upon. Mr. Campton reached into a file drawer by his desk and pulled out a form. "Your mother says she'd rather you have what we call in-school suspension. In other words, you'll stay confined here, away from your classmates, for the next two days in either my outer office or down in a guidance room. It'll be effective tomorrow first thing. How does this sound to you?" he asked.

"Doesn't surprise me," Monica said, "I guess she doesn't want me home. I don't care. I don't care about nothing." The hardened tone was back in her voice and she stopped crying.

"Excuse me, Mr. Campton, it's my planning time and I've got to run off a test. I would like to say something to Monica before

I leave." I faced Monica and leaned forward. "I've been angry with you many times in the past, and you know why. Monica, don't confuse my anger with hatred. I don't hate you." Neither of them spoke as I left the room and closed the door.

I felt awful that evening. Monica would probably hate me more than ever as a result of her suspension, and so would her friends. I was discouraged. "God, I asked you to draw us closer and I really believed You would, up until today. Why did it have to be me who caught her? Now, I might as well give up trying to reach Monica."

I was content to do just that until Romans 8:28 crossed my mind, "And we know that God causes all things to work together for good to those who love God, to those who are called according to His purpose."

The word "all" haunted me. All meant Monica. All meant this smoking incident. All meant my relationship to her and establishing peace in her class. I was encouraged by the verse, but even more so, by a God who had enough concern to work this situation into something good. While I thought about the problem I had a special, unusual feeling that Monica was receptive now. Somehow I knew that God wanted me to approach Monica during the suspension, not wait until later to talk with her again. It seemed like the worst possible timing to me, yet I was willing to try. "I'll go to her tomorrow, Father," I prayed, "but You're going to have to supply the words to break down her resistance."

It was a restful night. I woke up the following morning and prayerfully maintained the desire to talk with Monica. Crazy as it seemed, I felt hopeful and even eager to face her one-on-one. The only thing I feared was my own vulnerability. What if I had misread my own feelings? I would either come away having accomplished something positive, or I would get an earful of spiteful remarks. It was a chance I had to take.

The early morning hours passed quickly at school and my planning time came. I stopped by Mr. Campton's office to find out where Monica was stationed. "I know she hates me, Bill, but maybe I can make some headway with her today. She's got two whole days on her hands to think, you know."

"Go ahead and try if you want," he replied. "Remember, though, you're setting yourself up for failure if you expect the impossible. Her problems go back a long way."

"Wish me well down in the guidance annex," I answered and took one final breath at the office door. "Here I go."

The expression on Monica's face when I walked into the tiny room conveyed surprise and disgust. She was sitting alone at a table with a stack of closed books in front of her. "Oh, it's you," she said and turned away.

"Monica, I'd like to talk with you if that's all right." I pulled out the extra chair and sat down across from her at the small table. She intentionally looked toward the wall and didn't speak.

"Monica, is that all right?" I waited.

After what seemed like an eternity, she flipped her long hair back over her shoulders and answered, "Why would I want to talk to you? I hate you!"

"I wanted to talk to you about English. We can talk about that, can't we?"

She continued to stare at the wall.

"I'm open to any ideas you have that will help me improve the quality of instruction in our class. What would you suggest I do? Are there some things you would like to see me try? Are there things you don't like?"

Silence.

I continued, "You know, Monica, I'd really like for you to pass my course. I don't want you to repeat it in summer school or next year."

"Why are you bothering me? Haven't you done enough?" She didn't sound indignant, only solemn.

"How about the unit we did on Poe? I think most kids liked it, but how about you? Or did you prefer something like the play *The Miracle Worker*? Which?"

"Why don't you just go away?" she asked. For the first time she turned her face from the wall and looked at me.

"Monica, why aren't you trying to pass English? You didn't fail language arts last year and your teacher told me you ought to be producing much more than you are for me. Your guidance folder supports that too. Why is that?"

"I ain't talking to you."

"If you could change one thing about our class, what would it be?" Her eyes turned from me to the pile of books. She looked like she was thinking.

"Can you come up with one thing, Monica?" I waited.

"You go too fast," she said. She was actually responding to me like I was a real human being!

"How? How do I go fast?" I asked.

"You just do." Her voice wandered off and I felt I was losing her again.

"Can you give me an example? Is it in literature, grammar, or what?"

She didn't answer.

"Say," I wondered, "did you have anything to eat this morning?"

She shook her head back and forth. "I don't hardly ever eat breakfast."

"I didn't get a chance to eat this morning either. Would you mind if I got us a couple of donuts? They have some next door in the faculty lounge, even the big and gooey kind. It'll only take a second. Want one?"

"Why do you want to get me a donut? No, I don't want any."

"Come on, Monica," I said gently, "don't you think you'd feel better with something in your stomach? It's not all that nutritious, but let me get you one. My treat?"

"I can pay for my own. You don't have to buy anything for me."

"You can pay if you like, but it's fine if you don't. Now I'll be back in just a minute. Do you have any preference?"

She shrugged her shoulders. "They got any with nuts and icing?"

"I'll see."

I flew into the lounge and grabbed my purse for change. There were three or four teachers conversing. "Is the building on fire?" one asked.

"I can't explain much now," I said and picked out two nutty donuts from the large assortment, "but I'm not leaving the guidance room next door until Thomas and I can have a decent conversation. I've got to rush. Tell Linda I'm short a quarter."

Within minutes I was back and seated in the room with Monica. "Here," I said, "take your pick."

"That one," she said and pointed to the glazed Danish twist.

I handed her a napkin and sat down. "All those books in here make you look like some kind of scholar. Did you bring them or were they already here?"

"Only these two are mine," she said, "history and math."

"Are they your favorite subjects?"

"Don't know," she sighed.

I took a bite of my donut. "This thing is really loaded with nuts. How about yours?"

"It's all right."

"Do you have enough to keep you busy down here?"

"Yeah, I guess."

"Was your mother upset yesterday about the incident in the rest room?"

"Yeah." She didn't offer any more information and I didn't want to press the issue.

"What do you do in your spare time? Any hobbies?" I asked.

"Just listen to my stereo, watch TV, and party."

"What's your favorite show on television?"

"Look," she said and wiped her hands. "Look, why are you doing this? Why are you down here? Trying to con me or something?" She was calm and definitely not belligerent.

"I'm going to tell you because you asked, but I want you to really listen."

"What do you want from me?"

"The reason I'm here is because I'd like to show you that you matter and that you're important. You are. Do you understand?"

"I hear you."

"Monica, I want to make my class a successful experience for you. I want you to pass because you *can*. And, if I can go ahead and say something even though it's none of my business, I care about your family situation and how it must hurt."

I'd touched a sensitive nerve, and she turned her head from me.

"You don't know nothin'," she said, almost in a whisper.

"I know I care about you." I heard her attempt to laugh as though she'd heard this speech before from someone else.

"Monica, you just asked me a question and I tried to answer it as honestly as I could. Now I'd like to ask you one. Monica, why do you hate me?"

Her head bowed a little, ashamed and humbled by my question.

We sat silently for a couple minutes. She stared at the floor and I frayed a napkin as I thought and prayed. My planning time was nearly over, and it was apparent Monica wasn't going to respond. Perhaps she couldn't. Perhaps she didn't know how.

I got up from the table and walked to the door. "Monica, maybe it would help if you realized I'm on your side. No matter what you've thought before, I'm on your side. Think about it, please?"

Our relationship would never be the same again. I don't mean to imply that we all lived happily ever after (such simple endings are fit only for fairy tales). There would be times of disappointment ahead when Monica briefly lapsed back into old attention getting behavior. She never stayed there long, however, and with the gradual passing of the school year, she became one of my most faithful students.

"You should have heard Thomas talking about you in music last week," a teacher said one spring day.

"Oh?" I was a little embarrassed to have teachers in the lounge stop their own conversations and listen to ours.

"She thinks you're the greatest thing this school's ever had."

"Are you sure it was Thomas?" I asked in astonishment.

"You bet. I heard her with my own ears. Congratulations! You're the first adult she's ever liked."

Another teacher chimed in, "How did you do it, Campbell? How did you win her over?"

I paused to reflect. "I kept after her. Boy, did I keep after her! And I prayed a lot," I answered. "Underneath her stone exterior, that arrogant disposition, the cheating and everything else, she really hurts. She hurts a lot."

Today when I remember my first year of teaching, I think of flowers, gifts, and a funny cream pie in the face that were a part of my last week. Yet nothing affected me quite as much as one scraggly, misspelled letter. It was from Monica, and it was the only praise I ever received straight from her.

When I think of her now and when I get discouraged with more hardened students who come my way, I pull out her letter again. I let her words soak deep inside. "Love," she signed it, "and your friend always, Monica Thomas."

If I cry now, it's out of joy.

Thank you, God, thank you. Amen.

2

Burnouts and the Jesus Film

Of all the different kinds of students I met my first year, I suppose I had the deepest concern for those who labeled themselves burnouts. I'd heard of baseball strikeouts, tire blowouts, and even factory walkouts, but student burnouts? That was a new one.

Those who used this slang were so open and often boastful about their personal lives that it didn't take me long to figure out the word's meaning. A burnout was a regular user of drugs and one who was "burning" from the inside out because of the drugs' effect. The user could either "solo" this indulgence or "party" with friends in a community experience.

Burnouts were so diverse in social status, goals, behavior and abilities that it was hard for me to come up with generalities about them. Some were wealthy, others were not. Some were withdrawn, others were overactive. Some were dulled in thought and speech, while others were impressively alert. The common factor was an interest in drugs for pleasure and escape from boredom, home life, or feelings of worthlessness.

As my year unfolded I had a growing rapport with quite a few students who spoke to me freely about their drug activities. Even though I guessed that about 8-10% of my kids were actually burnouts, my classes arrived at higher figures when I asked them to appraise their freshman student body. I was stunned by their conclusions. The lowest estimate came from my first class. They judged unanimously that about 20% of the ninth graders regularly used drugs. The highest answer came from my fourth group. All agreed that 70% of their classmates partied from weekend to weekend! Whether or not their statistics were accurate, who could ignore them?

The more settled I was with my teaching duties, the more earnest I became in prayer. I was troubled by what I heard and saw in the lives of some of my students. Specifically, I was worried about my first few classes within which I sensed a higher concentration of drug users. I was worried when Ruth, a frail and pretty girl, quit school after weeks of physical trembling. I was worried when Sam, totally unaware of his actions, vomited all over himself, his desk, and books from mixing alcohol and drugs before school started. I was worried when Carrie, a bright and talented girl, was restrained on the floor where she fainted until her parents and doctor could be notified of the sudden hysterics.

The problems were much bigger than I, and so were their solutions. More than anything else I wanted to share the hope which God could give, yet I knew that I could never openly say those words in the classroom setting. I was hired to teach English—so I must not use Room 310 as a personal platform to preach and push my faith.

Then how could I stand out from any other average teacher? Was it even possible? If I were to make a difference, I reasoned, it would have to be in the way I lived and conducted class. Perhaps with sensitivity and enthusiasm I could encourage my students to ask the right questions, seek me out, and even desire the One who lives within. Not just burnouts who were often foremost in my mind, but anyone.

One of my favorite Old Testament verses had always been Isaiah 6:8, "Then I heard the voice of the Lord, saying, 'Whom shall I send, and who will go for Us?' Then I said, 'Here am I. Send me!' " I pondered that verse for a long time one evening during devotions and decided that I, too, wanted to be useful in touching lives at a deeper level. It was a golden turning point in my Christian walk when I prayed, "Father, like You called on Isaiah at his offer to be sent, call on me to be used here. I don't have to see the results, I just want to be useful to anyone who is receptive. I'd like to make an eternal difference to some—even one!—of these kids. Give me opportunities to share Your love with them, please? I'm serious. Here I am, use me."

I prayed those words for a solid week, and each time I became more and more fervent. Nothing out of the ordinary happened. I continued to pray for even the tiniest open door to share God's love. Still nothing! "Father, You're the most important person I could ever share. You could make the difference. Please? Could I be used by You and for You, even this week?"

The following day began as any other. I kept my classes busy with transparency notes on stories and authors. I remember backing away from the overhead projector to add a few last minute notations on the board. As I stretched out my arm in a sweeping gesture (I was always prone to get carried away), the chalk flew from my hand onto the floor. The kids burst out laughing and so did I. "Well, let me try that one again," I said and leaned down for one of the crumbled pieces.

If I'd found a million dollar bill I wouldn't have been more startled. There, beside my file cabinet and within the reach of my hand, were two huge film tins. The titles on the containers were in large capital letters, "The Life of Jesus Christ."

"Wow!" I exclaimed out loud. "I don't believe it!" I placed the films eagerly on my desktop.

"Did you find a Christmas gift or something?" one student joked.

"Close to it," I answered, trying to restore calmness to my voice. I pulled one reel from the can. "I still don't believe it!"

The students had no idea what was going on. They didn't realize how close to tears I was at having found something God planted in my room. How could I explain this precious, precious gift?

"Hey, are we going to see it?" Tom Briggs asked.

I continued examining the film and labels.

"Miss Campbell?" Tom stated firmly. I looked at him. "I asked if we were going to see it."

"I sure hope so, Tom."

"It must be pretty good if you're that excited," he remarked with his wide devilish grin.

"What can I say?" I smiled back, still amazed.

The bell rang and the students scampered out. I was grateful that immediately following class I had planning time alone. "Father, I'm overjoyed! Sally must have left this here by mistake, or I'd never have known about it. Please help me get clearance to show the film to my classes. And thank You so much for the discovery."

My first stop was the lounge to find Sally. She taught a course called The Bible as Literature in my room each morning to juniors and seniors. She herself wasn't a Christian, but she had a surprisingly naive ability to select evangelical books and materials for classroom use. Maybe the same luck would hold true for the film. I hoped so.

"Here you are," I said and shut the lounge door. "Sally, I found your film in my room a few minutes ago. What are the chances of showing it to my kids? It might give them some reference to choose your course later on. And besides, we could use a break."

"It's fine with me," she answered. What a relief! "The only problem is that it's rented and has to go back in tomorrow's mail."

"What time tomorrow?" I asked.

"You'll have to talk with Miss Meige about that. All I know is, I'll be through with it when it's your turn for the room."

"I'll drop down to the library and see what I can do," I responded. "It's days like this when I wish we didn't have the strictest audio-visual policies in the state! I hope she'll okay it, even if it is at the last minute."

Miss Meige was scolding a group of students when I walked into the library office. "God, please change her heart," I prayed. "Please help her to go along with the idea."

The students filed by me after their lecture on acceptable behavior. "Miss Meige?" I said. No one ever called her by her first name. "I was wondering if you could give me some information on a film that's here today. It's called 'The Life of Jesus Christ' and it has two parts."

"Yes, I remember. It's checked out for the Bible Lit. course. What about it?"

"I was . . . I was wondering if I could use it for my classes.

You know, a change of pace and all that. I've never seen it, but I'm sure it's good if Sally picked it out."

"That's strange. Don't you have freshmen?"

"Yes."

"I don't see how it fits," she said protectively.

"Well, it doesn't exactly fit, but I'd still like to use it. Sally said it was all right with her."

"Why would you want it though? Are you doing a unit on the Bible or something like that?"

"That's a good idea." I paused. "But no, I'm not."

"I think the film has to go back tomorrow. I go to the post office every single day at quarter of twelve. It seems to me you'll be cutting it close just to show it to your first two or three classes." Miss Meige wasn't thrilled about any special arrangements. I could tell by the tone in her voice.

"Two or three classes would be fine with me. Those are my roughest kids." I was beginning to stammer, "And . . . well . . . I don't know how to say this. The only time most of them have ever heard the name of Jesus it's been in vain to curse someone. They don't even know who Jesus is or why He came."

She stared at me and never spoke a word. Her right eyebrow was arched high.

I continued, "Please let me show it. It may be the only time any of them are exposed to the gospel."

She tapped her pen on the counter top.

"I know we're not supposed to duplicate another class' material," I said, "and that we're supposed to sign up for equipment at least three days in advance, but it means a lot to me. I'll even take the film to the post office myself during lunch if you like."

"Well, you can't have it two days, that's out. The school gets fined if the postmark isn't just so."

I was too afraid to say anything now. Maybe I had pushed too hard.

"This *is* irregular, but all right. All right. If you want it, you've got it until noon."

"Bless you," I said, "bless you!" She was startled when I shook her hand impulsively. "I won't forget this."

"Just remember that film better be on my desk by 11:45."

"Don't worry about a thing. I promise it'll be down here." I felt so happy I was ready to do cartwheels out the door. "Thanks!"

"You never did say...." her voice trailed off.

I stopped at the door and came back. "I didn't say what?"

"With only tomorrow and three classes, what part are you going to show?"

"Part 2, of course. I sure hope it does justice to Christ's death and resurrection, you know."

She was strangely embarrassed at her lack of words.

"Thanks again, Miss Meige." I turned and left.

The hours between the approval of the film and the time it would be shown were crucial. I called a close friend as soon as I arrived home after school. She shared my excitement and pledged to be in prayer with me for my students' receptive hearts. "And don't forget," I said, "that in an upper middle class school system like mine, parents can really raise a fuss if they think anything's offensive. I think we need to pray for God's protection and blessing all the way around. I'm not out to offend anyone," I finished. My friend agreed with me.

I slept very little that night and used the time for a special vigil. I prayed for each student by name, the classroom atmosphere, my own motivation, the quality of the film and it's portrayal of Christ. "Father, use it all to draw these kids to You. It could be ten years from now when one of them remembers something from the film. Maybe it will be the first link in a long, long chain for some of them to accept You. Thank You for letting me have a part in it. Thank You for wanting to use me."

What an exciting morning! I jumped out of bed, got dressed and gathered my teaching books in record speed. I don't think I'd ever been as eager to face a workday as I was that one. School didn't come fast enough!

The first things I looked for when I entered Room 310 were the film cans and projector. "Everything's all set," Sally said on her way out. "I'll just leave the projector here for you and I assume you'll get the film downstairs in time?"

"Yes, I'll be sure to. Miss Meige already knows about it. And thanks."

My class entered the room and asked a dozen questions about the film. I was busy threading Part 2 in the machine when I answered, "Good deduction! Yes, we're having a film today. I thought you kids deserved a break. Or maybe it's your teacher! Who knows?"

The tardy bell rang and I quickly took attendance from the

back of the room. "I'm going to give you a choice today. We can continue where we left off yesterday, or we can see a film instead. First let me tell you something about it.

"It's one of the films that is shown in an upper level English class. Some of you might want to take The Bible as Literature course in a couple of years, and this film is a sample of what to expect. I personally haven't seen it, but I understand it was produced recently. The title of it is 'The Life of Jesus Christ.'

"It's your choice. If some of you prefer not to see it for any reason, then I'll be happy to give you a pass to visit the library. If enough of you don't want to see it, then we can move on to other things."

All but three boys voted in favor of the film. "Come on, now," I said. "Is my teaching that bad for you to respond so overwhelmingly?"

"Yes!" they shouted. We all enjoyed the laugh.

I gave the passes to the boys who preferred to work on their algebra. "Here you go. I guess I'll see you tomorrow. Oh, could you get the lights on your way out? Thanks."

I turned on the projector. "Father, I wish they had stayed. Clark especially. He's going through a lot right now with his parents' divorce. Anyway, bless all of us here now. Help us focus our attention on You."

Part 2 began with the death of Lazarus. It appeared to have been filmed on location in the Holy Land with some famous actors in the principle roles. That would help spark interest in the students. The story followed the Scriptural accounts with little variance, and I was quite pleased.

I watched the class closely for any reactions. No one slept. No one talked or laughed. All eyes were on the movie screen. "If only the others had stayed," I thought. "I really wish they could see this. They need it."

The door cracked open and in the hallway light I saw three youthful figures tiptoe into the room. They returned! "What happened!" I whispered to Clark. "Did you have problems getting into the library or what?"

"No," he answered. "We just decided to come back."

"Do you want to go to the cafeteria study hall instead?"

"No, we'll stay here."

"Fine," I concluded, "you only missed about seven minutes of it."

The three friends walked to their seats while I stood in the back of the room rejoicing. "Thank you, God. They've come back."

The film was excellent, but my mind kept wandering off to the events of the past week. I could hardly believe that all this—the kids, the film, my own involvement—was real and not a dream. For once I felt that I was a part of something far more important than the everyday business of teaching in the public schools.

Three classes quietly, reverently saw the film that day. I watched a few students wipe a tear from their eyes during the dramatic scenes of the crucifixion. I witnessed some momentarily turn their heads away during Christ's humiliating trial and scourging. And I remember one boy's "All right!" when Jesus came back to life.

Time had never been better spent in Room 310. The groundwork was laid for future talks with searching students.

Even burnouts.

Especially burnouts.

Thank you again, Father. Amen.

3

Suzanne

"Excuse me, Miss Campbell," said a short, thin, blond-haired girl.

"Yes, Suzanne? What can I do for you?" I looked up and smiled.

"It's about our book reports. Do you think this one is acceptable? I didn't get it from our library at school; I found it." She handed me the paperback copy.

"Oh," I said. "Katherine Kuhlman's *I Believe in Miracles*. How did you happen to be interested in this one?"

"It's a long story," she replied.

"Well? School's officially out," I said. "Why don't you have a seat and fill me in? It's hard to find time to talk with you during the day."

"If you're not busy." She looked down at the pile of work on my desk.

"This can wait." I shuffled the papers and closed my briefcase. "Now what's on your mind?"

She pulled up a chair and sat down across from my desk. "I'd just like to know more about healing."

"Isn't it a fascinating subject? Some people believe in healing and others swear it's impossible and outdated. What do you think, Suzanne?"

"I don't know," she answered. "I'm almost all the way through the book and I think there's something to it. At least I hope so. Can I ask you what your opinion is?"

"Sure, if you remember I'm responding as one friend to another and not as your English teacher."

She nodded yes.

"Well, I'm not trying to avoid your question, but I don't think there are any pat answers about healing, no matter what people might say or write in books. I really do believe God can heal, Suzanne, sometimes dramatically all at once and sometimes through slower means like medicine, doctors, nurses and hospitals. Is either way less a miracle? I don't think so."

She looked very puzzled. "Why aren't some people healed when they ask God?" she stated.

"I don't know. Maybe their motivation is all wrong. Maybe they think the pennies in God's hand are more important than His hand itself. Or maybe God has a better plan which hasn't been revealed yet. Sometimes when we read books and hear sermons on healing—or any subject—we get the feeling that there's supposed to be one surefire formula that fits everyone and gets instant results. Kind of like a cookie cutter. Plunk. Plunk. Plunk. Is healing really all that simple? Are we? Is God? I can't believe it for a second."

"But don't you think some healers can pray a miracle into being?" she asked.

"Have you ever read through the New Testament?" I replied.

"I read part of it a long time ago."

"Jesus' disciples were involved with healing all the time, but do you know something? They were never motivated by cash, TV appearances, or notoriety. They were gripped by human suffering. And the most important point—they realized it was God who healed, never themselves."

"Are you saying everybody's phony, Miss Campbell?"

"Not at all. Not at all. I guess what I'm saying is that it's God who heals. People can pray with us, doctors can treat us, yet I think the healing process goes right back to God."

"I think I understand," she said. "That's kind of what Kuhlman says in *I Believe in Miracles.*"

"I'm glad to hear that, Suzanne, I really am."

Suzanne picked up the book and laid it back down. "I'd give anything to meet her. I hear she lives about a three hours' drive from here. Do you think she'd answer if I sent her a letter?" she asked.

"I don't have any idea. If you really want to, give it a try."

Suzanne seemed uneasy and troubled. "You see, Miss Campbell, I'm a severe diabetic. I have to take three and sometimes four large injections of insulin each day. My doctors keep increasing the dosages every few months, and I'm in and out of the hospital all the time. I'm so ashamed; look at my stomach."

She stood for a second and pulled up her T-shirt three inches. There were needle marks everywhere, and the texture of her skin resembled the roughness of an orange peel. Even her flesh tone seemed discolored.

She sat back down.

"I had no idea, Suzanne. How long have you been a diabetic?"

"Only a few years. I've read that diabetics can sometimes go blind. I'd rather die than be blind, Miss Campbell. I wouldn't want to live then. I couldn't." She brought her hands up to her face and began to sob.

It was important that she have these minutes to release the tight bands of fear. "It's all right, Suzanne. It's okay. Just let it out."

She took a deep breath and quieted down. "Anyway, I thought if I could get to see her," she pointed to the book, "then maybe a miracle could happen to me."

"I understand why it's important to you, I really do," I answered. "But I want to repeat something I said earlier. There just aren't any pat answers. Don't be easily swayed by people who tell you there are. Promise?"

"I'll think about what you said while I finish the book," Suzanne replied.

"That would be super. Be sure to let me know what you learn. Maybe if I get time this summer I'll try to get a copy and read it too."

"Then is it okay if I use it for class?" she asked.

"It's fine with me. I wish you well, Suzanne. Even before you shared this with me I could tell something was different about you. In a positive way. I think you've always impressed me as more mature and sensitive than others in your class. I never knew why until now. You've had a lot to handle."

"Thanks for letting me talk to you. I know you were busy no matter what you say."

"Anytime you want to talk . . . keep me posted."

I called several different friends that night to find out more information on Katherine Kuhlman. I had heard of her before, but my memory of her literature and public appearances was quite sketchy. On my third try I learned the news: Katherine Kuhlman had died some time ago.

Suzanne had to be told before she built more false hopes. "Father," I prayed that night, "thank You that I was with Suzanne today. That I could listen. That she valued my comments. Help her not to be too disappointed when she learns about Kuhlman's death. No matter what, Suzanne needs You. Maybe You can use the illness to draw her closer to yourself, I don't know. But if she's the slightest bit receptive, please use me to make a difference. Somehow I'd like to give her another book to read. Something to make her think. Would You help me pick it out?"

My eyes scanned the hundreds of books along my bedroom walls. "This is the one, Father, this is what I'll give her," I said and pulled The Hiding Place from the shelf. Many lessons came back to mind as I flipped through the pages of Corrie ten Boom's book on her World War II experiences. What an incredible story of faith in God and His protection! No other book but the Bible had ever spoken so much to me personally, and I was sure it could be meaningful to my young friend.

I was delighted to see Suzanne the next day in class. "If you get some time after school, drop by. I'd like to give you something," I told her. She assured me she would.

It was a hectic Friday full of tests and lectures, and I almost forgot about Suzanne until she entered my room. "Oh," I remarked, "is it time already? I've lost track of everything trying to get ready for our upcoming play. Come on in!"

"You always seem so busy, Miss Campbell," she said.

"I suppose I am most of the time, but not too busy to stop and talk with you kids. That's been the greatest reward of my first year here," I said.

"Don't we get in your hair a lot?" she asked, so seriously. I threw back my head and laughed loudly. She joined in. "Does that answer your question?" I teased.

I motioned for Suzanne to sit down as I fumbled through my briefcase for The Hiding Place. "I was thinking about you last night, Suzanne. I even called a couple friends to find out more information on Katherine Kuhlman. I've got some bad news for you," I said and looked directly at her.

"I think I already know what you're going to say. I heard it before, but I just thought it was a rumor. She's dead, isn't she?"

"A heart attack I heard."

"That's another lousy idea," she mumbled and looked toward the windows.

"What do you mean?"

"I just knew it was too good to be true. Just when I was ready to believe in God."

"I know you're upset, but you can work it through," I replied.

"You don't really know me, Miss Campbell. My friends and I nickel and dime it every single week," she said boldly.

"Do drugs help you cope with your diabetes, or do they only complicate your health?" I asked.

"I don't know how else to make it."

"Suzanne," I said and checked my watch with the room clock, "I'm due on stage down in the theater in about three minutes, so we won't be able to talk much longer. There are a couple things I'd like to say though.

"I like you. You've got a lot on the ball despite what you think about yourself. I was looking over my bookshelves last night and came across one of my favorites. I know you like to read, so I thought I'd bring it along to school and let you look at it. Here it is." I handed the book to her. "It's about one woman's real-life struggle for sanity and courage in World War II. She was a political prisoner in the concentration work camps. Want to read it? Want to give it a try?"

"I guess it sounds all right."

"Believe me, it's worthy of a second and third reading. I just love it. It starts off a little slow, but stick with it."

"At least it'll give me something to do. Are you sure it's really all that good?"

"Come on, Suzanne, trust me! You'll love it!"

"Okay, if you say so."

We talked of light and frivolous things on the way down to the theater. I felt good in my heart that Suzanne had sought me out the day before. I was excited by such a vital and open opportunity to be a part of her searching. Perhaps in years to come the message of *The Hiding Place* would return to her memory and fulfill a critical need. I had no idea. In the meantime I would continue to pray for her. I was compelled to.

It was a week or more until I saw Suzanne again. I had heard through the guidance office that Suzanne was sick. What I didn't know yet was that she had been readmitted into the hospital for further tests to balance her sugar and insulin levels. Apparently, during an argument with her father, she had poured her medicine down the kitchen drain. It was a terrible thing to do, and one which had immediate repercussions on her health.

She was out of the hospital one week later and back to school. Her class had not met that morning, so I was naturally surprised to see Suzanne dash into my room during my planning break.

"Miss Campbell! Miss Campbell!" she exclaimed. "I've really got to talk to you!"

"Hi, Suzanne," I said. "Welcome back! How have you been?"

"I'll tell you all about that later because I can't stay long. I'm supposed to be in math."

"You better hurry then. I don't want to keep you from someone else's class."

"You know that book you gave me? *The Hiding Place*?"

"Yes, of course, I remember. What about it?"

She was talking so fast it was difficult to understand all her words. "I finished it the other day in the hospital. I was bored to tears and then I remembered the book you gave me. Guess what!"

"What?" I said anxiously.

"I asked God to come into my life just like He did for Corrie and Betsy."

"Why that's wonderful! That's just great!"

"Yeah, I know. It's like I feel different already."

"That makes my day, Suzanne."

"What got to me was Corrie's peace. She held on to God in all that suffering—I couldn't believe it. Then what she said to everybody in the camps started getting through to me. I guess I wanted that closeness with God like she had." The joy on her face was obvious. Something *had* happened!

The elation and gratitude I had that week and those yet to come were inexpressible. My after school role soon became that of a listener as Suzanne continued to share her questions, discoveries, and doubts about her new life. It was a marvelous work God was doing in her, and I was honored to be such a direct part of it.

Suzanne moved with her family at the end of that month to a distant city. She kept in touch by letter for a while and she even phoned me a couple of times to talk and ask for prayer. It's been several years since I've heard from her. I don't know where she lives anymore, whether she's well, whether she's growing in Christ. I do know that I continue to pray for God's hand in her life.

I met Suzanne for a short time and then she was gone.

Father, keep her safe. Keep her from harm. Amen.

4

Butter, Anyone?

Very early in my teaching career I learned a simple yet profound lesson: if I really longed to be used by God, then He would open up the areas of service. Whether the opportunities were big or small, I didn't care; they were chances all the same for me to make a difference, to reach, to plant seeds. What a new dimension this added to my teaching!

I was blessed by my students over and over again that first year. I'll never forget the surprise of receiving six different cakes on my birthday, the array of Easter flowers, and the handful of cards for every holiday. The highest compliment I believe I ever received was when one class, then another, wanted me to go out with them for supper. Would I escort them, they wondered? Would I take time to go?

"Do you think I want to be seen with you guys in public?" I said. "You've got to be kidding!" Yet deep inside I felt terribly honored.

We decided to meet at an area steak house inside a nearby

shopping mall. Between the time I said, "Yes, I'll be there," and the actual evening we went, my students intimidated me with all sorts of crazy notions. "Bret's going to tap dance on your baked potatoes." "Alice will 'woo woo woo' the manager into a free meal for you." "Victor's going to serenade you with his bass drum." Worst of all, they threatened to burp, at the same time, on the count of one, two, three. I didn't know for sure what to expect, but I did know we would leave our mark.

It was a thrilling experience to walk through the large glass doors at the mall's entrance and see at least twenty of my students from one class huddled around the spouting fountains. There was a mass of hands waving to me in the distance, urgently reminding me to hurry and get in line. It would be at least twenty minutes before we inched our way to the woman who took orders.

"You gonna treat us?" a voice in my long and winding line shouted back.

"So sorry," I returned, "my bank was closed. At least I tried! How about if I spring for dessert?"

Twenty little "yeah, yeah, yeah's" went back and forth.

"Not here," I said. "How about afterwards? We could walk across the mall and get ice cream cones."

Their response was unanimous and immediate. "Shhh," I reminded, "we seem to be attracting attention."

"Are you kids here for a convention or something?" one kind gentleman asked.

Before I had a chance to respond, two of my students admitted, "No, we're just here tonight to eat. *That's* our English teacher. We decided to bring her along." I turned red when they pointed to me.

It took forever to get our meals and find twenty seats relatively close to one another in the crowded restaurant. The private banquet room was filled, but two huge round tables in the regular dining area were available. When all the formalities were over—earth shattering issues such as who sits where and *what do we do with all these coats?*—an incredible thing happened. Nearly everyone at my table lifted up their plates and pulled two or three butter pads out from underneath. I glanced at our other table and saw more students doing the same thing.

"Butter, anyone?" Brenda shouted across to us. "I got plenty." Many people's attention was drawn toward us.

"What are you talking about?" I whispered and made a sign with my hand. "A little quieter this time."

"You tell her, Victor," Brenda said. "You're sitting closer."

"Victor?" I asked suspiciously. "What's up?"

"It's like this, Miss Campbell. Butter costs 3¢ each and we like a lot of it. If you slip the butter pads under your plate like this," he was now demonstrating, "no one will ever know and you can save money! Ha—isn't that pretty sly?" he said.

I raised my voice so that all my students could hear. "Come on, why don't you go back and pay for them? It's not going to break you up. Besides, don't you know you're stealing?"

"It's only butter. They'll never miss it. They must get at least a thousand customers in here each day!" Brenda shouted back.

"But it's stealing, Brenda," I said, trying to keep my voice low.

We talked more among ourselves and I realized all my persuasion wasn't doing any good. "Okay, I'll drop it for now, but we're going to talk about this later," I said.

The meal and comraderie were excellent as we relaxed and enjoyed the conversation. We discussed practically every subject under the sun, from Jiminy Cricket's fan mail to strapping a bomb under my chair at school. Our levity was good-natured and healthy.

We left the restaurant and walked through the mall a while, discussing all the new, clever ways to skip classes, "borrow" the family car, or stay out late at night. We were a funny sight—twenty-plus-one licking away at our cones while we shopped.

Time passed and we eventually had to go our separate ways. "See you tomorrow," I said. "I have one more important stop to make before I leave, and then it's home to type a test."

I waved good-bye and headed back to Towne's Steak House. It was nearly empty now.

"Excuse me. Is the manager here?" I asked the same attendant who took our orders earlier that night.

"Sure, Miss," she said. "Right over there." She pointed to her right.

I walked over to the man in the blue suit. "Pardon me, but could I speak with you for a second if you're not busy?"

"What can I do for you?" he said cordially.

"I'm a teacher in an area school district, and some of my

students and I dropped by for dinner here tonight."
"Was everything all right?"
"On your part, superb. We had a little mix-up on our end though. It had to do with the butter."
"Butter?" he asked.
"Yes, butter. Some of my kids hid butter pads under their plates and didn't pay for them. They didn't *intend* to pay for them."
"I see," he said, still unsure of my purpose there.
"I don't know about you, Sir, but I'm a Christian and I don't believe in stealing, even little things. Those were my students . . . and . . . well . . . I'd like to give you the money to make sure what they took is actually paid for."
"That's very commendable of you, Miss, but I suppose—"
"No, I really want to do this. It's the right thing." I laid the money on his table and started to leave. "Oh, and Sir?"
He looked at me, scratching his head. "Yes?"
"Have a good evening." I walked out the exit.

Honesty is important to me and I wanted to stress this idea to my class. With God's help I could make a positive statement and an object lesson that would make my students think twice before they stole again. There was understandably a new warmth between that particular class and me because of our meal together the night before. We would return to law and order, we would work harder on the tasks at hand, and we were more united now. Closer. A tighter inner circle.
"Before I begin class today," I told them, "I have a couple things to say about last night. I'm sorry some of you couldn't make it because all of us had a good time. I really enjoyed the evening, especially the ice cream cones and our window-shopping.
"There is one more thing." I walked over to my desk, the place of authority. "You remember that business about the butter under your plates?"
A few students chuckled and looked at one another. "Ah!" I said. "You *do* remember!
"I don't want to belabor the issue, and this is the last time I'll ever bring it up. I know the butter only costs 3¢ each, but when you guys take twenty or more of them it adds up. If you're faithful in little things, you're going to be faithful in big ones.

And the reverse of that is true if you're not faithful. Know what I mean?

"Anyway, I want to fill you in on last night. After you left, I went back to the restaurant and paid for the butter you took. If you want to cheat me out of the money, that's all right. I don't care. But I couldn't stand by and watch you cheat someone else. Big or small, stealing is still stealing. Think about it."

We went on with class as usual. No one ever mentioned the butter incident, yet I'm sure by the pensive expressions on my students' faces that my speech was heard and that it made an impact.

"Chalk it up as a little lesson," I told myself.

I had almost forgotten the episode altogether until the last day of school. One boy, Victor, wrote a letter on the back of his semester exam.

Dear Miss Campbell,

I may forget the stories, books, grammar and everything else you tried to teach us, but I will never forget that night at Towne's Steak House. Not the meal, but what you did about the butter we took.

I've gone to the parochial schools all my life and I have heard a lot of talk about honesty. But you, Miss Campbell, were the first one to ever show me.

I'll never forget it. I think your faith is real.

Sincerely,
Victor

Lord, it pays to be faithful in little things. Amen.

5

Abbey and the Mickey Mouse Watch

Fifteen years old. Reasonably intelligent. Poised. Uniquely pretty. That's how Abbey appeared on the surface at first glance. In reality she produced the least amount of effort needed to get by. She felt worthless, hopeless, and craved the very attention she turned away. Abbey worked hard at withdrawal from anyone or anything that might involve risk. She had learned quite early in life not to trust.

Abbey was never a discipline problem, nor did she ever volunteer an answer in class to warrant a special response from me. I believe she would have come and gone anonymously every single day if I had let her.

I admit I was curious to learn more about Abbey. Since she resisted even my slightest effort to pleasantly converse, I decided to draw closer to her through her best friend Jill. Jill had many of Abbey's own attributes, but she was a little more open to communication and had not been as rudely disillusioned with life. As a pair they both seemed removed from the mainstream; they habitually wore heavy makeup and exaggerated Indian and astrological jewelry; and they always reeked with the smell of smoke.

I prayed for the two of them long before I attempted to know them better. Why were they so different? What were they really like? My goal was not only to help them successfully pass my course, but I would also try to instill some sense of worth in them at the same time.

"Jill, how about coming in before or after school, or even during my planning time, for some extra tutoring? I've looked over your comprehensive reading scores, and I think the extra work could bring you right up to par."

"I don't know," she answered. "Would it help my grade?"

"Without a doubt. We could even drill you for each of the weekly tests in addition to the reading exercises."

"How long will it take?" Jill asked.

"As long as you want. I only wish we had more time to work on this in class."

Abbey was waiting by the door for Jill. Wherever they went, they went together.

"Abbey is welcome to come too," I said loudly enough for her to hear. "How about both of you trying this as a team?"

Jill was the only one to respond. "I'll talk it over with Abbey and if we decide yes, we'll see you today after school."

They left and came back together at the end of the day. Still it was Jill who did all the talking when we sat down to outline material. Aside from shrugging her shoulders and "yes" or "no," Abbey never spoke until two weeks and four tutoring sessions later. During the fifth, we discussed a writing project which was due the upcoming week. It was a persuasion paper and was to focus on one important issue or problem in the student's life.

"Have you both decided on your problem yet?" I asked.

Jill, as always, was the one to respond. "I think I'd like to write about drugs or sex."

"Those are pretty heavy topics, Jill. What angle do you plan to take?"

"Probably the same as Abbey's."

I turned to Abbey. "And what might that be?"

"They're both fun but can mess you up," Abbey said to Jill without glancing at me.

"Then are you trying to persuade your reader for or against the problems?" I asked in a calming, gentle way. I definitely didn't want to respond in condemnation.

"For," Abbey said, "no, I guess against. They leave you pretty empty in the end."

"What do you think about them, Jill?" I was trying to open up a discussion among us.

"I think you got to do what you got to do," she responded.

"I hear what you're saying, but I'm not sure I follow."

"If the only way to feel alive is through the leaf, then you got to smoke. If the only way a guy will hold you is in the back of his van, then at least you get wanted for a little while."

"How about you, Abbey? What do you think?" I shifted the emphasis back to her.

"Like she said, at least you feel wanted."

"Don't you feel wanted?" I asked Abbey directly. They both looked at one another and I thought for a second they were ready to withdraw and leave.

Instead I was surprised by Jill. "My old man split and my mom's got too much to do to fool with me."

"Are there others in your family?" I asked.

Jill answered, "Three brothers. One quit school, one freaked out, and one's smaller."

"Abbey?" I said. "Do you have any brothers or sisters?"

"Just an older sister. I know my dad cares but. . . ."

"But what?"

"He's got an old war injury. He's paralyzed from the waist down. He works part-time in our neighbor's watch shop. . . ." her voice trailed off.

"Do you feel wanted, Abbey?" I asked.

"Yeah, I guess. I don't know. Yeah, I suppose so. But I wonder sometimes what I'm doing here."

"Here?"

"Alive. Why life's so hard. Why people just use you. Nobody really cares. Not really."

"That's a pretty big generalization, don't you think?"

"So it's big?" Abbey answered. "It's still the truth. We're just a couple of burnouts. Now who's gonna waste their time on us? Who's gonna trust us burnouts?"

"I enjoy spending time with you and I don't think it's wasted or that you're unimportant," I stated.

"You're just playing teacher," Jill replied.

"You don't think I'm concerned about you?"

The three of us paused.

I continued, "Sure I care about your performance in my class, but it doesn't stop there." Jill looked like she was listening to me. Abbey did not.

"What's troubling you, Abbey?"

"They're nice words, Miss Campbell, but what could you possibly want from us?"

"I'm not trying to use you if that's what you mean. Can't I be your teacher and friend at the same time? No strings attached?"

Abbey said no more and Jill seemed to be preoccupied with the last few statements. I concluded that neither of them had heard anything like this before and it was a hard concept to swallow.

Our session was over and the girls had to leave. They promised to do some more work on their persuasion papers and get back with me in a couple of days.

When Thursday came and they showed up again after school, I decided not to mention anything about our last conversation unless they brought it up. They didn't, so I let it pass for the next few weeks. We kept our attention strictly on schoolwork, and soon saw some progress made in their grades.

As time passed Jill and Abbey were more trustful of me. Abbey was still miles behind Jill and I was often worried about the isolated world she lived in. I hoped that she would lower the barriers between us, yet I never once felt that would happen until I somehow proved I trusted her in an extraordinary way. Otherwise, it would be pure, cold academics and nothing more.

I always had a sense of peace when I prayed for Jill and Abbey. I knew that someday we would have an opportunity to share again, but I didn't know when this would happen or how. "Father God, please make a way to reach them. Especially Abbey," I prayed.

Within a week I had the answer that would bridge the gap between Abbey and me.

I know it probably looked strange to a lot of people, but the most cherished possession I owned was an authentic Mickey Mouse watch. Ever since I could remember, I had always wanted one—rare, the adult size, more valued with age. When my sister gave one to me for Christmas years ago, I wore it constantly. Through high school. Through college. And now as a teacher. Because it was such a novel keepsake, it became a kind of trademark for me among my friends and students.

What had happened once in college, happened that morning while I readied myself for school—my watch broke. I sat on the edge of my bed and shook it furiously. I wound it. I wound it again. Nothing. It was definitely broken.

I recalled what I'd done before in college: spent a couple of afternoons on the phone trying to locate a watch repair shop that would work on it. No luck. I eventually had to return my watch to its original manufacturer, and it took six months to get it back. "Six months," I thought, "not another six months? How discouraging!"

The watch was in the back of my mind the whole day, and I'd foolishly wasted my energy sulking. When Jill and Abbey stopped by for their usual Thursday review I was a little less than lively. Then an idea sparked. "Say, Abbey! Didn't you tell me once that your father did watch repairs?"

"Yeah," she answered.

"Does he work on most brands?"

"I think so, but I'd have to ask."

I pulled out a sheet of paper and scribbled down the brand name and model of my watch. "Could you give this to your dad and see if he'll take a look at it? Dear old Mickey konked out on me this morning. Would you please remember to ask him tonight? I really love that timepiece."

The next morning I put the watch in my purse and hoped and prayed Abbey's father would at least glance at it.

"Hi, Abbey!" I saw her by accident in the hall at the change of an early morning class. "Did you ask your father last night? You know, about my watch?"

"Uh-huh," she answered.

"What's the verdict?" I shouted above the noisy confusion.

"He said he's done some work on that kind, and he should be able to clean and check it over," Abbey returned.

"Great!" I exclaimed. "Is his shop around here somewhere? I'll drop it by after school."

"It's about thirty minutes away, but you can just give it to me."

My heart almost stopped. For all my thoughts on trust, I was really afraid to let her take the watch home. What if it got lost?

What if someone stole her purse? What if she sold it to get money? She had to pay for her drugs somehow.

"Look," I stammered, "you're going to be late for your next class. We'll talk about it later, okay?"

"Sure," Abbey said and edged herself back into the hallway traffic.

I wanted to be sure on this one. When I was alone and had time to think over the situation I prayed, "Dear Father, only You know how much that watch means to me. I feel pretty silly to be worried over it, but I guess I don't trust any student to carry it around. It's not just Abbey. Remember when I had to send it through the mail and I insured it for $2,000? We both know it wasn't worth nearly that much, yet it seemed that valuable to me. I'm scared to turn it over because Abbey might lose it, and I'm scared not to turn it over because I might lose Abbey. She would know then for sure that I don't trust her."

I thought some more. My choice seemed risky but necessary. "Be with me in this, God, all the way. And please protect that watch."

"Abbey," I told her later that day, "I can't begin to put into words just how dear this Mickey Mouse watch is to me. There are a lot of memories attached to it," I said and looked down to where it rested in my palm. "I've never trusted any student with anything more valuable in my whole life. Abbey, you're important to me. That's why I'm going to trust this to you."

I held out the watch for her to take. She looked at me, then down at the watch, then at me again. Her hand scooped it up from mine. She opened her purse and put it inside without speaking a single word.

"Be sure to tell your dad that he should go ahead and fix it whatever the cost. Tell him to be gentle with it, Abbey." We looked at each other and smiled. Something important was happening. Something that all the speeches and sermons in the world couldn't accomplish.

"You'd better hurry on to history. Here's a pass just in case you don't get there before the bell." I offered the paper slip while she gathered books in her arms.

"See you Monday," Abbey said and stepped out the door.

I had determined not to hound Abbey for daily information reports on my watch. My eagerness might be misunderstood as a lack of trust, and I would wait as long as I could to hear the

news and progress. Finally, seven days later, she came into my room with a broad grin on her face.
"Hold out your hand," Abbey said.
"If it's what I think it is, I'm going to hug you!" I answered.
"Well, in that case...." she stepped back a foot.
"Okay, no hugs. I promise."
"Here you go." She plunked a green envelope into my hand. "Dad says there's no charge and it works perfectly now."
I tore open the envelope. I was beaming! "How can I ever thank you, Abbey? And your dad!"
"My dad says it's on the house. He won't take anything; I already asked."
"I'll send him a thank you note and drop by his shop. I'm so grateful! And say, why don't you, Jill, and I have dinner together some day next week to celebrate?"
"Where at?" Abbey asked.
"The mall is pretty close and there are several good restaurants there. Take your pick. Make sure it's all right with your folks first."
To my surprise Abbey and Jill both liked the idea. With their parents' permission I drove them myself from the school to the mall. Jill's mother would take them home from there.
"Woo! Fancy car," Jill said.
"Not really. Mine's in the garage getting fixed, and they gave me this silver streak, four-on-the-floor, jacked-up sports thing as a loaner. It looks nice, doesn't it? You just wait and see what happens when I 'rev it up' to get the clutch out—everyone in town will hear us take off."
They were impressed with the roar of the engine despite the fact that we were shouting to be heard. Thank goodness it was only a five-minute drive until we came to a halt. As soon as we got out of the car I met a couple of old college friends. "These are two of my favorite students. This is Abbey and this is Jill. I'm really proud of the work they're putting into my class," I said to introduce them. We chatted a while and moved on. Then Abbey spoke up. "They probably think you've flipped out to be seen with us."
"Why?" I answered. "I meant what I said. Now let's go to Devlin's and order."
We were comfortably seated and refreshed after a drink of water. Abbey and I sat quietly and watched Jill rummage

through her purse. "Mind if we smoke? We do at home; it's no surprise to anyone," she stated to me.

"It's your choice," I answered.

She lit a cigarette and passed the pack to Abbey. "No thanks, not yet," Abbey replied. They looked so much older now.

I asked many questions during the meal to help draw Jill and Abbey into a meaningful disclosure of themselves. They shared more pieces of their lives than I'd ever expected, and they seemed trusting at last. They could say what they wanted and they knew I was not going to condemn them.

"Ever experience a natural high?" I asked after one of them mentioned her regular use of marijuana.

"What do you mean?" said Jill.

"Do you ever feel that it's good to be alive when you aren't doing drugs?"

"No, can't say as I have," she answered.

"How about you, Abbey?"

"I don't know. You mean like with a guy and . . . you know."

"No, I mean all by yourself. Or maybe with God."

Jill interrupted. "Why don't you tell us what a natural high means to you?" She was serious and even put out her cigarette.

In the next ten or fifteen minutes I told them about myself, my own conversion as a college freshman, and how God had fulfilled many needs. All their attention was on me and they seemed to hear every word.

Abbey admitted she had gone to church earlier in her life, but then had drifted away from any belief in God. "I'm sure I'm no prize for God now," she said.

"Me neither," Jill laughed.

Abbey wasn't laughing.

"That's where I think you're wrong," I said. "You may give up on yourselves, but God? Never. You matter too much to Him."

Our meal had been finished half an hour ago, and I felt a change of surroundings and conversation was needed. The seeds had been planted and my prayers answered at last.

We spent another hour in the mall, walking through some stores and talking about all sorts of trivialities. We saw some cute Mickey Mouse drinking glasses and were reminded of our original purpose in getting together for dinner.

"My watch has worked perfectly, Abbey. Just about every

time I look at it I think of you and your dad."

"I'm glad it happened like it did," Abbey said.

"How do you mean?"

"Because I learned you weren't faking with all those nice words about trust. After all, we're just a couple of burnouts."

Jill and Abbey worked hard in my class and passed decently at the end of the year. To the majority of people they were still outcasts and nobodies. To me they were students whose lives I had tried to touch. To me they were individuals whose lives were worth touching.

May they find your love, Lord Jesus. Sometime. Somewhere. Amen.

6

Big Al, My Pal

I never initially feared any student quite like I feared "Big Al, my Pal," as I often addressed him. Alvin Quincy Martin Dazio was a six-foot-three-inch mass of towering flesh, complete with tattoos, earring, high leather boots, oil stained jeans and a black leather jacket which bore the famous skull and crossbones insignia. His hair was always a long mass of nappy, unwashed curls, and his body had the pungent scent of a sweaty locker room.

If this constant reminder of gutsy strength in the back corner seat were not terrible enough, add to the picture a large-linked dog chain that Big Al brought to class each day. When I bored him (a frequent occurrence because he had failed English the year before and during summer school), he would take the chain from his neck and use it like a jump rope on the top of his desk. Bamm! Bamm! Ching! Bamm!

"Excuse me, Big Al," I leaned forward, touched his shoulder and whispered.

"Yeah, Miss Campbell?" he returned with a half smile. Big Al always loved it when I called him by his special name.

"It's hard for me to talk up there when you're flipping your chain, you know?" I pointed to several others who sat around him. "And I think they're probably straining to hear what I'm saying when you twirl that round and round."

"Uh-huh," he grunted.

"Big Al, I really don't mind what you do with that chain back here, really I don't. But could you just keep the noise down?" I asked.

"I got'cha," he said and swung the chain around his neck. He would be mindful of our talk for a few more days, and then I would have to repeat the speech all over again, exactly as before.

I learned in time that my Goliath had a gentle nature despite his physical size and gruff exterior. Certainly not many of those who dressed in oil and leather would even listen to an adult, but Big Al was different: he was a loner. And simply because of this, I knew he could be reached.

Paul's words in 1 Corinthians 9:20, 22 became a meaningful tool for understanding how to relate to a lot of students, including Big Al. "And to the Jews I became as a Jew . . . to the weak I became weak that I might win the weak; I have become all things to all men, that I may by all means save some." Now of course I could not become my students or model their lifestyles, but I *could* show willingness to learn about their interests and find some common ground on which to meet. For Big Al, this meant understanding the grease under his nails. It meant sharing his love for fast cars and motorcycles.

I knew exactly two facts about cars: *this is a car, and this is a garage where I take the car to have it fixed.* My knowledge of cycles was exactly the same. I knew if I expected to earn Big Al's respect on my fast wielding terminology of motors and such, I'd have to do a lot better than that.

My first stop was at a magazine newsstand. "Can you show me what you've got on cycles and customized race cars?" I asked the gentleman behind the counter.

"Sure, Lady," he said out of the corner of his mouth, puffing all the while on a fat, stubby, unlit cigar. "Your brother in the hospital or somethin'?" He dropped a half dozen magazines on the counter before me.

"No, I just decided it was about time I learned a little more on the subjects, that's all."

"Then I recommend this one, this one, and that one," he said and pulled three magazines from the pile.

"I'll take these two for now, and be back if I need to know more."

"Suit yourself. I got to give you credit, Ma'am, for wanting to impress your boyfriend like this. That's downright American."

"It's not for my boyfriend," I returned politely. "It's for a young man in one of my English classes. His whole life revolves around bikes and cars, and if I ever expect to be heard I'd better speak his language and speak it well."

"He must be pretty special if you're going to all this trouble," the man said and put the magazines in a bag.

"I suppose you're partly right," I answered and gathered my change. "He *is* special—don't get me wrong—but I'd like to think that *all* of my kids are special too."

"Ahhh," he replied and raised his eyebrows as if he really understood.

"Thanks for your help," I said and nodded good-bye.

That night I sat down on the edge of my bed with magazines in hand. The more I studied them the more complex everything seemed. "Father God, I'll never be able to keep all this straight. One model over another. Engine power. Ignition systems and exhausts. It'll take me months to get this down pat and understand what I'm talking about. Please provide a way for me to narrow down all the alternatives for a discussion with Big Al. Show me where to begin and what's important. And God, in time help me reach him. Help me win his trust."

I pondered my magazines over toast the next morning, and I even packed them away in my briefcase for any spare seconds I might have to reread them during the day. For the time being I would concentrate on imagined conversations about this cycle over that one, and try to find some thread of logic that could pass Big Al's inspection.

It was not that day but the following one in which the temperature in my classroom soared well above the 85 degree mark. This would normally be a welcome change except for the fact that we were in the middle of winter, and all of us were naturally dressed in our warm wool sweaters and layered shirt tops. By the time second period arrived, and the sweat was running down my brow, I peeled off my suit jacket and vest. By third period I had rolled up the sleeves on my blouse as far as they would go. I honestly thought I was going to collapse on the spot.

There were more complications. Teachers in my wing of the building were told not to open windows until the janitors could locate the source of the problem. *What will the taxpayers think if they drive by on a snowy January day and see the third floor windows wide open?* In the meantime we panted, we raved and suffocated in the torturing heat.

With only five minutes left before my third class could leave, there came a dramatic cry from the back of the room. In desperation Big Al yelled, "I CAN'T TAKE IT ANYMORE!" And for the first time that year he unzipped his leather jacket and flung it off to the floor behind him. For a brief second as his head went down to rest on his desktop, I saw a word blocked in huge letters across his faded yellow T-shirt. It was "Suzuki."

"Thank you, Father," I prayed. "What a blessing this heat has turned out to be! Al's favorite cycle must be Suzuki . . . that'll make everything so much easier now that I know what bike interests him."

The boiler valves were repaired by mid-afternoon, but somehow I had the strange urge to wear my favorite summer shirt when I got home, and head right back out the door for an ice cream cone. I resisted both ideas and went instead to the telephone directory to look up area motorcycle dealers. I wasn't even sure any of them would be open for business. How could they sell cycles in winter weather?

"Bert Kudland's Cycle Center," said the voice on the other end of the telephone.

"Hello. My name is Jean Campbell and I'm calling for some general information about Suzuki cycles. I think the one I'm probably most curious about is the 150 or 250 class for motocross racing. What general features can you tell me about them?"

For fifteen minutes we talked about the uniqueness of their particular bikes over other brands with equal or more power. After I hung up, I returned to the now worn magazine on cycles and read the statistics of performance again. I even made a little list of informational points on an index card, and I used it as a study sheet for that night and the following days.

I waited a solid week until the moment of truth arrived. The hard part was not so much remembering what I'd put on the card, the real task was restricting Big Al to the limited number of topics I could discuss. One little diversion, one little sidetrack, and I would be lost.

"Say Big Al," I smiled and pulled out a chair along the back wall of my room. "Why aren't you taking advantage of the study time to catch up on your notes?" I sat down next to him and sipped away from my coffee mug.

"I don't think I'd pass anyway," he answered and scratched his arm through the leather cuff. It gave a crackling, squeaky sound.

"What do you wish you could be doing right now? You have a distant look on your face, Al."

"Racing. I wish I was outside right this minute racing. I got my license, you know. Bet you I'm the only freshman who drives himself to school every single day."

"You mean racing your car? That's what you want to do?"

"No, I mean on my bike. Moto-x. You can't do it on the streets, you have to go into the woods somewhere to practice. And I like it real good."

"What model do you have?" I asked.

"A Suzuki 250. It took me a long time to save up and buy it. I sure wish the weather would change. But not like the other day in here."

"Don't even mention last week's heat wave," I gestured by fanning my hand in front of my face, "or you might jinx us, and I don't think we'll survive a second time."

We both sighed in agreement.

"I've heard about moto-x racing, Big Al. I hear it's pretty dangerous because of the number of bikes competing at one time and the pressure of winning."

"Yeah, I seen some pretty rough things, but I guess I don't care 'bout dangers. That's what makes it fine."

"Where do you work on your bike? Does your dad help you in your garage at home or what?"

"No. Ain't got no dad. See, I got this part-time job at a garage down on Oak Road, and when I get off work they let me use their shop and tools and everything." He seemed proud of his after school efforts.

"Are you trying to get more muscle from your 250?" I said.

"Yeah. This spring I really want to be a winner. And then maybe trade up to a real powerhouse someday like the 370." I could tell his dream was real and deep by the way he looked beyond me to the white sky outside.

"Someone once told me that if I wanted to speed tune a 250," I said and cleared my throat, "I ought to start with the stock ignition. You know . . . replace the breaker points with a capacitor discharge ignition system. That way I'd get more complete firing at any RPM. Some bikers don't think there's much of a change with just that alone." I intentionally shrugged my shoulders to imply maybe there was, maybe there wasn't a real difference.

Big Al responded, "A buddy of mine went through 2 CDI's last season. They break a lot."

"I know what you mean." I tapped my finger on his desk-top for effect. "With all the new electronic ignitions, they need to work on getting the bugs out of those little magic boxes."

"Yep," he answered. I was definitely talking his language now. Some students scooted their desks around to watch us debate. Big Al added, looking back to me, "But if you install an expansion chamber and reject the carburetor for top-end and mid-range power, she'll run like a scalded cat. But then you have to go to a colder spark plug to keep from holding the piston."

"No doubt about it," I chuckled. "What a crazy way to burn out your engine!"

Big Al laughed too, and folded his arms.

I continued, "Isn't the real goal to get more fuel into the combustion chamber? I'd say the best way to decrease your ET is to take the ports and recut them."

He nodded yes. I added, "Now, if the ports were more finely ground and polished, you'd feel the extra snap you need and still stay in your 250 class. What do you think? You'd decrease your lap time by . . . oh . . . say 3 seconds. That would give you about a 1.5 second edge on a 30 minute moto. It may not sound like a whole lot to the amateur, but I bet it would make the difference between winning and second place."

Some of the boys who were listening to our conversation smiled from ear to ear, and they looked back to Big Al when I paused. One of them whispered, "Can you believe an English teacher—a *woman*—rappin' bikes?"

I went on as though I'd never heard his comment. "Of course that's not the only way I suppose you could improve your time. Maybe if you install a reed valve and mill .020 off the head, you'd have more bottom end and you could ride in other events. Say like the hare scrambles and enduros."

"Yeah . . . I seen some of them," he answered, "but I want to keep as close to stock as possible for long distance reliability."

"That's pretty much what the Suzuki factory teams are doing, and they sure are winning the races," I said.

"Did you see Joel Robert trophied first overall at Pepperell?" Al stated.

"Oh, you mean over in Massachusetts?" I asked.

"Uh-huh. Man, if I could ever copy his style. The way he shoots off the berm and crosses up off the jumps. He's the best!"

"From what I've read," I said and sipped more coffee, "there are lots of sports journalists who agree with your opinion. He's been labeled hot stuff for several years now."

We rambled another twenty minutes on Al's first love before we were interrupted by the high pitched ringing from the hallway bells. Class was officially over and it was time to go. While nearby students pushed and pulled their desks back into place, Big Al stood and stretched out his hand. I stood too, fumbled my cup to my left hand, and reached out with my right.

"I got to admit, Miss Campbell," he said while shaking my hand, "you really know motors. I never figured you one to know motors."

"Big Al, I don't know what to say," I returned awkwardly.

"How long you been hooked?"

"Hooked?" I asked.

"On cycles."

"Not too long. Actually I got interested when I realized this person I knew loved bikes. I wanted to impress him."

"Well you sure impressed *me*," Al said and walked a few steps away, his back turned toward me.

"I did?" I whispered softly with doubt.

"And tell that guy he's awful lucky to have someone care 'n go to all that trouble." There was a trace of sadness in his voice as he slipped out the door.

"I will, Big Al," I said in the quiet, empty room. "I'll share that *and more* . . . someday soon."

Father, you teach that everyone is important, everyone counts. Please strive with Al. Lead him closer yet. And Lord? Use me again. Amen.

7

Open Forum

"Mr. Ruppart?"

"Have a seat," the principal said and lit his pipe. "What's on your mind?"

"A lot of things. I hardly know where to begin."

"I've heard good things about your classes so far," he said.

"The inner city is certainly different from where I taught last year. *That's a fact.* Restraining the class of hellions I've got before lunch just may mean the death of me," I answered.

"What's the problem?" he asked and placed his hands behind his neck as a kind of headrest in his principal's chair.

"I'm working on them, and I suppose I'll win some of them over sooner or later," I said. "I really wanted to talk to you about something else."

"Oh?" he replied.

"I've been at this school a couple months, and it goes without saying that I've got a lot here to handle and a lot more to learn." I was nervously toying with my favorite fountain pen.

"Are you saying you wish you were back at your other school? Maybe you should have stayed there a second year before coming here?"

"No Sir, that's not it. I *wanted* to try some type of inner city work, and this system is the perfect size to get my feet wet. Having freshmen in a junior high setting has given me a whole new perspective on education, Mr. Ruppart, and coming here has also helped me appreciate kids of all races."

"Jean, I still don't follow," he said and relit his pipe.

"Trying to teach my students composition, grammar, and everything else that goes with English is one thing," I stammered and broke off. It was obvious I was having a terrible time.

"And what's the other?"

"I can't help but think there's something else I could be doing. Do you realize how many kids come from broken homes, how many have faced death and real tragedy in their families? Some with only one or two changes of clothing to their name? One student last week told me the only heat his family has is what comes from the kitchen when his mother lights old newspapers and magazines in the opened stove. Their electricity's been off for a month because they can't pay the bill."

Neither of us ventured to speak for a moment. I stretched my hand in an upward motion and took a deep breath. "I . . . I took a girl home the other day because she hurt her leg and no one could come pick her up. I swear to you my feet would have broken through the rotted porch steps of her house if I'd walked up to the front door."

"What are you really trying to tell me?" Ruppart asked.

"I know it's a long shot, but what would you say if I tried to get an after school fellowship group going in kids' homes?"

"What kind of a fellowship group do you have in mind?"

"A Christian interfaith fellowship. A place where I can sit down with kids eye-to-eye and share something which speaks to all this hurt."

"But how would it work?" he commented. "I don't understand."

"I'm not sure yet myself. Have you ever heard of Youth for Christ or Young Life Bible Studies?"

He gave a slight gesture that at least one of the names rang a familiar bell.

"I think I'll try to pattern my format after theirs," I said. "But I prefer to start off with girls. Mixed groups at this age level probably wouldn't work too well. We'll meet in homes away from the school setting. Involve parents when we can. Provide time for fun. Interaction. Listening. Relate to them that God can meet their needs. Maybe even throw in a little singing to help pull us together; I play around with the guitar in my spare time."

He leaned forward in his chair. "You really believe in all that?"

"You bet I do," I said with conviction.

"But who are you gearing this for? What particular faith?" he asked.

"I want it to be available for anyone and everyone. There are certain advantages if we don't use the labels of any one particular denomination. And by the way, I'm not intending for the fellowship to take the place of any church's youth group; I want mine to supplement whatever their program offers. I certainly don't want to get off on issues like how one church baptizes, how another offers communion, or analyze formal modes of worship. In fact, I *won't* get on them."

"Do you have any idea how you'll begin?" Ruppart said.

"I've already asked a handful of girls if they were interested."

"And what did they say?"

"They said yes. One student who lives two blocks away already volunteered her house. Lots of kids walk to and from school, what's another two blocks?" I stated. "Besides, I'd kind of like to visit from one house to another each week. We could involve more people that way."

"We've never had anything like that at our school before," Ruppart cautioned. "I'm not sure how it would go over."

"The way I'd want it—and probably the only way it would work—is to keep the group strictly separate from school. I won't use signs in the halls, announcements over the public address system or anything like that. It will be totally on its own, away from the classroom. I . . . I guess I'm not asking for permission. I'm asking for your blessing."

"I see," he said. "I see."

"My job here is to teach and that's what I try my best to do during the day. But after school? After school I want to provide a place where searching students can find deeper meaning to their lives. I know I won't reach everyone, but I want to try to make a difference."

"Whom do you have in mind?" he asked.

"For starters, try Colleen Zerbe and Mary Ann Dobbs."

"You think you can do something for those two?" he asked in surprise.

"I'm going to try," I answered. "All I can do is try. Most of the kids I've asked already have some religious affiliation, but there are others who'll come simply because I've asked them to."

"How soon will you begin?"

"I'm not sure. I was hoping to find someone else to help share the responsibility with me. Maybe another teacher, a church youth leader here in town, I don't know. I came to you ahead of time just in case any parents approach you. I don't think it's a conflict of interest if I do both. It shouldn't be."

He reached into his leather pouch and pulled out a pinch of tobacco for his pipe. "So long as you're not promoting it in your classroom and it's on your own time in the community," he offered, "it sounds all right to me. If you can reach a couple of kids like you just mentioned, more power to you."

"I'll do my best to keep you informed," I replied and got up from the chair.

"Good luck," Mr. Ruppart said as I left his office.

In the following couple weeks I prayed earnestly that God would direct me to someone else who could help bear the burden and concern of an after school fellowship group. And, as I had come to expect, God opened the door.

"Hi," I said. "You're new here, aren't you?"

The tall, slim teacher answered, "Yes, I just started this week. I'm filling in a few months for Miss Lincoln while she has her back surgery."

"How do you like teaching so far?" I asked. "The kids giving you a run for your money?"

She chuckled. "You could say that, yes. Definitely. I've never worked in a school like this one. It's different, but I guess it's good experience."

"Have you ever taught before?" I said.

"No, I'm just fresh out of college. My other job helps me some, but I need the extra money and I'm subbing when I can." I noticed she used her hands a lot when she talked. She had a warm, casual manner and it was almost like I'd known her for years.

"Oh? What else do you do besides teach?"

"I'm a youth leader at an area Methodist church. It's about a mile or two from here, not far from the expressway."

"You don't say?" I commented with a growing smile on my face.

"I don't know if you've ever heard of them, but I was involved with Campus Crusade for Christ during college. Then a few months ago my dad happened to hear of a youth opening at a church near here. I couldn't find a full-time teaching job and . . . well . . . here I am."

"That's great!" I exclaimed. "I think you're just the person I've been waiting for."

"How do you mean?" she asked.

"You wouldn't happen to be interested in helping me start a girls Christian fellowship group after school right in this neighborhood, would you? I'm very familiar with Campus Crusade although I was more in to Young Life myself."

"If I can squeeze it into my time schedule, sure," she said. "I'd love to discuss it more and give it a try."

"By the way, I'm Jean Campbell." I held out my hand to greet her. "I'm in English. Welcome."

"And I'm Kelsey Parks," she said, gripping my hand in a hearty handshake. "I'm in music. Thanks."

I had often felt that God's best presents came in the form of friends, and this was undoubtedly true with the special prize of Kelsey Parks. Not only did we share our common goal to show—not just tell—God's love to kids, we also drew close as one young Christian to another. Laughing over dinner. Playing ping pong and racquet ball by our made-up rules for days on end (or so it seemed). Reflecting on our lives into the early hours of the morning with open Bibles before us. Discovering the joys of a mutual Father. Kelsey Parks was a beautiful, precious gift.

It took about three weeks of planning and organization before she and I were ready for our first meeting of the After School Fellowship Group. We had the small band of eight interested girls select a night which suited each of them and agree on whose home we would visit first. They voted for Thursdays and, to get us started, Sally Black's place.

"Ready to go?" I asked Kelsey on the front steps of Sally's house.

"Just relax, Jean," Kelsey reminded. "God will take care of everything."

"It's just that I've never been this vulnerable in front of students before. Speaking to teens at various churches, yes. Students in a group from school, never. One-on-one I could handle, but a group?"

"It'll be all right. You'll see."

"Kelsey, if anything goes wrong, you can go tra-la-la-ing off to some other school and sing your heart out. I've got to face these kids tomorrow and the next day and the next."

"So you're taking chances, Jean? Chances they'll see your openness and spread it around school? God can handle that too."

"I know you're right, Kelsey. I'm just scared."

We said a quick prayer and Kelsey rang the doorbell.

When we were escorted to the living room and refreshed with a glass of punch, we sensed the awkwardness of people meeting people for the first time. Several of the girls had not known one another except by sight at distances in the crowded school halls, and only two of them had met Kelsey in music class.

"I think it's time we introduce ourselves," I began. "Let's start with you, Sally. Fill us in on what you like to do, your hobbies and so on, okay? You and I know what they are, but Kelsey and some others might not know."

After we had come full circle we leisurely talked of school, the pain of English homework, current movie stars, newly released albums and the various pre-holiday pursuits that would fill our weeks before Christmas. The more we talked and laughed, the more at ease we felt with one another.

"How about going around the group for one last quick question?" I asked. "Both Kelsey and I genuinely want to tailor this fellowship to meet your needs. Could you give us some of your ideas on what you hope to gain by coming? What topics could we prepare discussions for? How can we help you?"

The general consensus was for a little bit of everything, a kind of religious smorgasbord. We were to provide time for comic release, have a serious portion for discussing problems, doubts or questions, and offer some sort of instruction from the Bible.

Maybe even go places together. "Whatever you think's important, Miss Campbell. Really. We'll go along with what you two decide," one girl assured us.

"Let's get back to this later," I said. "We only have about fifteen minutes before most of you have to leave. Kelsey and I wanted to conclude our first gathering by telling you how we became Christians. It may not mean too much to you now, but maybe it'll make more sense as time goes by this year, or ten years into the future.

"Kelsey, why don't you go first? Maybe give us a little background on yourself and what you're doing with us today."

"Well, Jean . . . well, kids . . . I'm here because my Christian commitment is what makes my life worth living. I didn't always think that. I guess everything initially became real for me back when I was about your age.

"I was the only child in my family, and I grew up as a very self-sufficient young lady," Kelsey said. "I was content with my life and I never saw that there might be something dramatically wrong. One night as I was drifting off to sleep I remembered a scavenging fox I'd seen earlier that day about four feet from me in the woods. Anyway, I fell asleep and had a terrible nightmare about a sick and rabid wolf that was attacking me right in my own back yard.

"I woke up totally panicked in a mess of twisted sheets. I don't think I'd ever sweated and been so afraid before in my whole life. I know it might sound strange to you, but I was shocked that I'd gotten so upset over a lousy dream.

"The reason I was so scared was because it was the first time I had thought seriously about death. I was afraid to die. Me. To die. Cool, calm, collected Kelsey Parks afraid to die. It was a piercing thought.

"For once in my fifteen years I realized I wasn't worth a whole lot to people the way I was. What could give my life value? What could add depth? I thought of a hundred unrelated answers to those questions but they were meaningless. All meaningless. And then, almost out of nowhere, the thought crossed my mind that I needed God as my savior to take away my fear of death. I needed Jesus Christ to keep me from living such a hollow life.

"I'd never been religious. No one in my family was. I'd gone to a church but nothing had ever sunk in. It's like I went through all the right motions and said all the right words. Everyone had been fooled. Even me.

"I lay back down that very same night and prayed a simple prayer, asking God and His Son to come into my life. To forgive me. To give me a new hope for Heaven. It's hard to explain, but something was different inside me instantly. I sensed it then and I sensed it the following morning. It was like God gave me new eyes to see with, a new heart to love with.

"I hope as this fellowship group shares together over the months ahead that Jean and I can point out the changes and joys that have come to us. Perhaps these joys will be yours, too.

"Jean? You want to take it from here?" Kelsey asked.

"Fine," I answered, "except I'm not sure I know where to begin.

"Kids, I get asked a lot by friends, teachers, and parents of students at school how I like my job. You know something? As much as I like what I do, I don't *live* for teaching. I don't get up in the morning to teach, and I wouldn't put my life on the line for it. Teaching may have value to me, but it's not all-important. My relationship to God is what I consider all-important and that's why Kelsey and I are here with you right now."

I paused to reflect a few seconds and continued, "I didn't have a storybook childhood like my friend Kelsey. My family wasn't down-and-out poor, but we never really had a lot. I was the youngest in a family of four kids and we had our share of problems . . . but it seemed like each member always faced them alone.

"About the time I was heading for junior high, my parents were beginning a long and trying divorce. My dad was an alcoholic and my mother's health wasn't the best, so you can understand how the whole thing was pretty unnerving for me. In fact, I was terribly, terribly insecure. For years it felt like I didn't have any support system at all.

"I suppose by the time I was a freshman in college I might have looked 'together' on the outside with decent grades, lots of impressive activities, a college scholarship and some awards I'd picked up along the way, but inside I was dying. I was desperate to find some direction for my life. Did I matter to anyone? I mean *really* matter?

"An English teacher in college sensed my searching and

realized how much I was hurting inside. She frequently shared her faith with me and told me that God could fill the deep longings I had. If she hadn't pulled me aside, if she hadn't shown me I was special to *Someone,* I don't think I'd be around today. I wasn't afraid of dying, kids, I was afraid of living. I was afraid of being a nobody with no purpose and no significance. A meaningless face in a crowd of millions.

"I left college one day in the middle of the afternoon and drove home. I went straight to my bedroom and began to weep. 'God, if You're there and if You're real,' I prayed, 'then I give You my life. I've tried anything and everything to fill this emptiness and I've gotten nowhere. I don't believe in You like my teacher, but I have no place else to turn. If there's anything left to salvage, take me. I'm Yours.'

"Kids, if you never hear another word I say the rest of this year, hear this: turning myself over to Christ that February evening was the beginning of a new life for me. God gave me a clean slate and a reason for getting up in the morning. Not all at once, but gradually He pulled me up out of despair and turned me around. If He could do that for me, then He can do it for you. Don't ever forget that.

"Several of you have already asked me why we'd be interested in spending time with you like this. It's because Kelsey and I want you to know we care about you and, moreover, we want you to know that God cares about you. We believe God can make you a whole person—strong and tall—to meet the circumstances of your lives. We really do."

I looked down at my watch. "The time has gone so fast. Let's close in prayer," I said and bowed my head.

"Father, only You can fill the emptiness in each of us, the wandering, all our aimless pursuits and the countless questions that haunt us day and night. You are the answer to our deepest longings.

"I pray that you will pull us together as a tight inner circle of friends who care for one another. Thanks for each of these kids. For Kelsey and what she means to me. Father, Your love has made all the difference in my world. This is the simple message I bear. In the spirit of Your Son I pray. Amen."

As I reflect on my first year as a group leader, I would be hard pressed to isolate one particular meeting or one individual girl's experience and state that it was more meaningful than the others. The truth is that we were *all* affected. The truth is that even today, several years later, I still receive visits and letters from the same band of impressionable young women who quite literally set the pattern for future groups.

Kelsey and I faithfully continued our Bible meetings in students' homes, and we retained the original eight through the ups and downs of winter weather, spring fever and girls track. Kelsey left our group at the end of the school year and was replaced the following September by a young black woman who taught history. Serving as a new team member, Carolyn Huntley was instrumental in providing Christian leadership for blacks at our junior high and in the Bible fellowship.

Although all of the freshman girls left us for the high school campus when they became sophomores, Carolyn and I enjoyed an increase in the group's attendance our second year. We were blessed by growing support from parents as well as an area church that graciously volunteered its building for our special activities. In fact, we were met with positive appraisals at every turn of our spiritual adventure except one. The only resistance we encountered came from fellow teachers who protested that we spent too much time with our students. *"You mean you like to be bothered after 4:00? But how does that look for the rest of us?"*

What an understatement to say the best is yet to come. I pray that when I stand before my God in heaven, I'll be surrounded by the youthful friends I tried so hard to reach on earth. I pray that at the great eternal gathering of the ages, our original circle of shared lives will be forever unbroken.

So be it days without end, Father. Amen.

8

Shame

It may not always be obvious to outsiders, but I'm basically a lazy person. Oh, I don't just have the kind of sluggishness that causes me to toss my possessions to the four winds, or the kind that regularly allows my bedroom to be a helter-skelter mess of clothing, books, and—God forgive me—dust. I mean a deeper kind of inactivity that all too often lets me be comfortable with the status quo . . . a slothful absence of motivation . . . a carefree complacency which permits life to go by untouched.

I was enjoying such a prolonged period of casual ease when God taught me a lesson I would long remember.

"Say, Jean, can I see you a second?" Ted Collins asked.

"Sure, Ted. What's on your mind? The math department in need of a little refining?" I answered.

"Don't get cute," Ted laughed, "or I'll get my brother to dig up your tax returns. You know, the one who works for the IRS?"

"Come on, Teddy Collins, you'll have to think of a better threat than that. Besides, you don't think your department needs refining? You don't think it needs—"

"Truce!" he interjected and threw up his hands. "We'll pick up on this later when I have time to defend myself. As it is, I've got to be downstairs for a meeting in two minutes."

"What can I do for you then? In two minutes or less?"

He grew serious and stated, "It's about a girl you've got in study hall. She really needs help."

"Who?" I asked.

"Willis. Gwendolyn Willis."

"Ahhh, little Gwen," I remarked. "Such a tiny girl. What about her?"

"I've got her for basic math, and she is totally spaced out. I don't know what's going on, but she has deteriorated this last month like night and day. Her appearance. Her total withdrawal. The way she stares into space."

"Ted, I don't understand. I only have her for forty-five minutes every other day in a study hall situation. What can I do?"

"Can you talk to her? Can you find out what's going on? You're better with kids like that; they don't feel as threatened and they'll open up."

"I suppose I can ask Gwen," I said. "It won't hurt to ask."

"Just see what's going on, all right?" he urged.

"I'm not promising any miracles, but I'll try to work it around tactfully. Now that you mention it, she has been looking ragged."

"Ragged? She looks like she's aged ten years in three weeks!"

I pointed to the wall clock. "You're going to be late downstairs. You better scoot. I'll see what I can do and get back to you."

One week later Ted Collins found me down in the cafeteria, leisurely chatting with some of my English students at their lunch table. "Miss Campbell, can I talk with you outside?" Ted asked.

"Why don't you join us? We're just discussing the odds on tomorrow's game against Washington," I said. "What's your opinion? Can Weak-Knees Knoll here save our team?"

"Thanks, a lot, Miss Campbell," Bill Knoll laughed from his end of the table and shook his head. "How good are you at catching a tray full of french fries from where you're sitting?"

"Uh-oh, Bill," I teased, "if you put it *that* way—"

"Miss Campbell," Ted interrupted, "I don't have much time." He motioned in the direction of the cafeteria doors. "Outside a minute?"

"Excuse us, kids. I'll be right back, and I expect that Bill will have finished all of those fries—grease and all—by the time I return!"

Ted Collins and I walked out the lunchroom exit.

"So what's up, Ted?"

"It's about Gwen. Have you talked with her yet?"

I sighed and tapped my palm to my forehead. "I'm sorry, Ted. I forgot all about it."

"I was hoping you had at least tried," he answered with disappointment.

"I'm really sorry. It just slipped my mind."

"Pete told me they called her down to Guidance this morning and couldn't find out a thing. Something has to be wrong."

"I promise I'll look into it this time. I really will."

"Please? For her sake?"

"Yes," I answered and waved hello to a boy passing in the hall.

"I'm just concerned, that's all."

"I know, Ted, and so am I. I'll try to see her as soon as I can."

"Okay, Jean. I'm holding you to that."

"See you later," I offered and walked back into the noisy cafeteria to find my table of sports enthusiasts.

Days passed and I did nothing. I noticed the dark circles under Gwen's eyes, the hands that shook, the loss of weight, the constant gazing out the windows, and still I did nothing. Somehow I had convinced myself to wait for the right moment (whatever *that* was) to call me to action.

Even though Ted never asked me again about Gwen, his presence around school was a constant reminder of my awful procrastination and broken promise. And there were other unpleasant reminders, too. Gwen's name seemed to be a frequent topic of conversation and rumor in the faculty lounge; her face often hung in the back of my mind during my long drives home; and I even dodged around her several times in prayer. "I'll get to her, Father, really I will," I stammered and moved on to other issues of greater importance. Things like: *What should I wear for my Sunday speaking engagement?* or *How can I possibly visit Beth Ann Saturday when I've promised to babysit my niece? and God, could you help me remember where in all this mess I put my favorite fountain pen?*

The occasion on which my comfortable, unruffled, balloon-like world burst was a Friday right after school. I was monitoring the hall outside my room when a frail and sickly girl slipped through the crowd of students, flying coats, and crashing lockers to make her way to me. It was Gwen, and she half-gestured for me to step back into my room.

"Hi, Gwen!" I said. "I've been meaning to talk with you for weeks now. I guess today's the day."

"Here," she mumbled and handed me a blue sheet of paper. Her voice was shaky and I noticed that she did not look up at me.

"What's this?" I asked in surprise.

"Transfer. I . . . I'm leaving."

"But I don't understand. Where are you going?"

"Across town."

"Your family's moving?" I asked.

"No. I am."

"Gwen, I still don't understand."

"Across town to . . . to . . . to the class for girls."

What a shock to suddenly see the pieces of her closely guarded secret fit together. Little thirteen-year-old Gwendolyn Willis was pregnant.

"Gwen, please look at me," I said and touched her shoulder.

She continued to stare at the floor in disgrace.

"How long have you known?"

"A month maybe. I finally told the school nurse here this morning. I had to after my doctor visit with Mom yesterday."

"But Gwen—"

"Miss Campbell, I got to go. They're waiting for me downstairs. I'm sorry we never had time to talk before. I always hoped I'd get you when I became a freshman. Now . . . well, now I guess I won't have the chance."

"I don't know what—"

"You're supposed to sign right down here," she said and looked up long enough to point to the only vacant space on her transfer sheet.

I initialed the slip and returned it to her. "Gwen, you don't know how I wish—"

"Really I got to go, Miss Campbell. My mother's mad enough at me already."

Before she turned and walked away, I clutched her free hand in both of mine. "I'm so sorry, Gwen. I'm so, so sorry."

"Yeah." She paused, looked directly in my eyes as though she were going to say something else.

"What is it?" I asked.

"If . . . if only you wasn't so busy. I . . . I was trying to build up my courage to tell you."

"Oh, Gwen," I struggled to say as the finality of her transfer and words pierced deep within.

She pulled her hand from mine and slowly walked back out into the noisy hallway. Numb, I watched Gwen make her long and lonely journey down the corridor.

It was hard driving home that afternoon because of hot tears which blurred my vision. The humiliation and shame I had witnessed on Gwen's face were now on my own for a much different reason. How could I have been so preoccupied with a thousand unimportant things that I let that opportunity pass by? How could I have been so content in my own little world that I ignored the obvious hurt in Gwen's?

I cried the evening away, especially when I remembered Christ's words in Matthew 25:40, "To the extent that you did it to one of these brothers of Mine, even the least of them, you did it to Me." It was close to midnight when I could finally venture the painful healing of prayer. "Father," I wept, "how I must have let You down. I'm so ashamed. The truth is that I waited much too long to help someone else. All those hints of Gwen. All those reminders day after day. The tugging of your Spirit. I ignored them all.

"Father, I hate this lazy, self-sufficient attitude of mine. We both know I would have let it go on and on until something else jerked me back to reality. Suffering this evening for my own shame is one thing, but letting Gwen suffer for weeks alone in hers is another.

"Maybe nothing would have come from my drawing close to her, but at the very least I could have listened. I could have said I cared. I could have said *You* cared. Forgive me, Father. I don't know if anything else redemptive can come from today, but I pledge right now to never wait long to reach out when I see a need again."

Although I turned out the light and tried to sleep, I found myself extremely restless. Finally I got up, cleared a small space on my bedroom desk and pulled out one of my stationery boxes. "Maybe it's too late for this, yet I ask Your blessing as I try to write Gwen. Guide me, Father, and make each word count."

I eventually managed a finished letter on my third attempt. Twice before a teardrop here and there made the ink on my paper form blotchy, irregular shapes. In a page and a half I told Gwen that I would miss her, that I was sorry I never got to know her better, and I concluded by sharing that even now, God loved her and could get her through the adjustments ahead.

It was finished. An incredible amount of release came through that letter, and I knew my effort would be cherished by Gwen for months to come. Perhaps, in another time, with different circumstances, we might pick up our relationship and build on what was started here. Remote as it seemed, this was still a hope I would pray for during the weeks ahead.

My life continued much as usual after that eventful Friday, but deep inside I knew I had been changed. I was certainly humbled by the incident with Gwen, and I grew from it. As a result I think I learned to talk a little less, listen a little more, and wait upon the Father with a new quietness of heart.

The story of this young girl is not over. I was amazed to receive a letter from Gwen's mother four months after the transfer. She updated me on her daughter's health, the process of finalizing plans to adopt the baby themselves, and Gwen's natural fears at giving birth. The bulk of her message, however, was thanks.

"I don't know why you took an interest in Gwendolyn," she wrote, "but we appreciate it. She's read your letter a hundred times. We are grateful you gave her something to hope in and someone to trust. It's a special gift to be able to inspire and encourage teenagers these days, and I think you've done both with our Gwen."

In answer to my prayers God gave me a second chance to draw nearer. Weeks after I received her mother's letter, there came another one, this time from Gwen's twenty-year-old sister. On behalf of her family, she invited me to join them for a baby shower and birthday party they were intending to give.

The sister signed her card with: "P.S. Our mother would really like you to come and visit Gwen. It would be good for her to see you now and we know you could ease her mind. Please come."

Unlike before, this time I would listen. This time, I would take advantage of the opportunity to meet with Gwen. This time I would gladly drive the distance to her home. And this time God was able to give me a deeper sensitivity to other girls I'd eventually have in class; who, for whatever reasons, found themselves pregnant and alone. I learned they would need compassion too, not criticism. Forgiveness, not greater burdens of isolation and added guilt.

Little Gwendolyn Willis pulled through her trauma of childbirth, and although I've never seen her since, I occasionally receive brief messages from her or about her. I have no doubt that her road is always a hard one to travel. Even now I'm sure her life is continually full of regrets, longings, and insecurities.

I'm sorry to say that Gwen has not yet found the freedom and forgiveness in Christ, but she is young. I would not be unexpectedly surprised to learn that someday, somewhere, someone else was able to build on what was started a few years ago when Gwen sat in my study hall and then left so abruptly.

Whether our paths will ever again cross, I do not know. But I know I tried to make a difference. I tried to understand.

And for now, that is enough.

Lord Jesus, only You can turn shame into something good and useful. You have done that for me. Please do it for Gwen. In Your name. Amen.

9

Benny

Miss Campbell, I got to talk. Can I come in?

What a surprise, Benny! Well, sure! How did you ever find out where I live?

My cousin knew someone who had your number. We finally traced your address through the phone company. I figured if I called, you might not let me come over.

It's a little late in the evening, but you're welcome to come in. How long will you be in town?

A week or so. I'm staying with relatives about twenty miles away.

Here, let me take your jacket. Sit down.

What time is it?

Close to 9:30. How'd you get here, anyway? You don't have your own car yet, do you?

Naw, I got my cousin's. Actually, I'm driving on my temps.

Benny!

It's okay. Honest. I've been driving like this for a year.

And you've never been caught?
So far so good!
Can I get you something? Hot chocolate? Tea?"
I could sure go for a Coke.
Let me check. I'll be back in a second.
Hey, whatever made you live so far away from school?
You'll have to speak up, Benny. I can't hear you!
I said, I was wondering why you live way over here and not close to school!
I guess I kind of like the distance. When I see that "End City Limits" sign I feel freer, separated from where I work. Besides, most of my family and friends live in this town so I never felt like moving away.
You got a nice place. And there's that rug you were telling us about in school last year.
It took me a while to make it. Designed it from a little two-inch drawing. I did everything by hand.
Well you sure blew it up big enough. I like it.
Do you want a lot of ice?
Whatever you got is fine with me, Miss Campbell.
Here you go; just set it on this. Pepsi's all I had.
Mmm. Tastes good. Thanks.
You sure you want to drink that stuff so late? You'll be up all night!
Doesn't matter to me none. I . . . I can't sleep too well anyways.
Benny, I've got to ask. Just after your family moved last spring I heard some bad news about your brother. Benny, is it true?
Yeah, what a shocker. It's true.
Can you talk about it? Can you tell me what happened?
Some of his friends went partyin' and Mitch tagged along. I guess they got to drinkin' pretty heavy. And when they were coming home, some guy in the car started fussing with Mitch. Mitch never took nothin' from nobody, so he told Bruce—that's who was driving—to pull over.
Benny, are you okay?
He told Bruce to pull over and they got out.
We can talk about something else. This is upsetting you too much.
Mitch, he ain't never carried a weapon in his whole life, but

this other guy flashed out an eight-inch knife. And he . . . and he . . .

Benny, it's all right. You don't have to.

Mitch . . . he . . . he died right along the road . . . his face buried in the gravel. Bruce said the other guy went wild and wouldn't stop. Couldn't even pull him off. He says Mitch kept screaming JESUS, JESUS, JESUS! He says he'll never forget that scream as long as he lives.

Here, Benny, use this. Just relax. Don't try to talk for a while.

My brother, he never hurt nobody. He didn't deserve to die. Not like that. Not over something stupid like that. My brother was good. He was good, Miss Campbell.

Benny, how's your mother? How's she taking all this?

I don't know. Some days I don't think she'll ever snap out of it. Sometimes she says she can't take it anymore. Says she'll pass on.

And your sister?

She just got back. She ran away for about a month. Down south. She doesn't look so good.

How do you mean?

I've taken drugs, Miss Campbell. But I ain't never taken drugs like Sissy. She's pumped up full of them, and Mom says she'll turn her out if she can't straighten up.

Can she, Benny? Can your sister go straight on her own?

I don't see how. She worries me real bad.

Have you told her that?

She don't hear when I talk.

Is there anything you can do to help?

When Sissy gets going, she says the cruelest things to Mom. I smack her . . . I make her stop. We can't take any more tension; we're all going to explode wide open.

Benny, how about you? What's holding you together?

Together? Together? Am I holding myself together?

Why haven't you run away like your sister? What's keeping you in one piece?

Don't know. Maybe Mitch. Maybe wanting to help my mother for him like he always did. He loved her, you know. And he took over just like a man when our dad split.

Have you heard from your father?

You kidding? Haven't seen him for five or six years. Wouldn't know him if he came up on the street and said, "Hey, Kid! I'm your daddy!"

It upsets me, Benny. It hurts me to know you've been through so much.

I guess I came to really ask you one question, Miss Campbell.

And what's that? What can I answer?

Why?

Why? Why Mitch? Why is Sissy like she is and my mother close to taking her own life? Why? I ask that a hundred times each day. Why? Do you know?

Benny, I don't have the answers.

But why, Miss Campbell? Why?

Can I read you something? It's in that book on the stand next to you. Hand it to me, please.

A Bible?

A Bible. Here's the place. 1 Corinthians 13. It's often called the great love chapter. Maybe you've already read it yourself.

What does love have to do with this? Can it bring Mitch back? Can it give Mama strength? Or me? Sissy?

There's a small verse toward the end of the chapter. Let me read it to you. It says, "For now we see in a mirror dimly, but then face to face; now I know in part, but then I shall know fully just as I also have been fully known."

I don't get it.

Let me repeat part of it again. Listen closely. "For now we see in a mirror dimly, but then face to face; now I know in part, but then I shall know fully. . . ." Some things can't be comprehended here because, at best, we look through a foggy glass. But then? Then means in eternity. Then means in Heaven.

Do you think Mitch is there?

You ask me hard questions. Maybe he knew Jesus. Maybe he was calling out for Him late that night in pain, Benny. If he knew Jesus, he's there.

Do you think Mitch knows why?

I'm not sure, but I'm certain God does.

Why would God kill my brother?

Benny, God didn't kill Mitch. It's hard to say why He allowed it—we're back to the foggy glass again—but He didn't cause it. God isn't cruel and this wasn't some awful joke He was playing on you.

I miss him. I miss him so much.

I know you do. And I know it hurts. It's not easy to lose someone you love. It never is, even under the best of circumstances.

All this talk of Heaven. Do you think it's for real?

Yes. And I think that whatever joys we find there will far outweigh any sorrows we've gone through here. At least that's what the Scriptures say again and again. Even the loss of your brother can't be compared to that kind of joy. Even the turmoil in your family right now.

My family . . . what am I going to do?

All that you have to do to stay afloat. You can make it, Benny. As impossible as it looks, you can make it.

I don't have the strength anymore.

I didn't say you'd make it on your own strength.

What do you mean then?

Maybe it's time you call on someone else.

What—you going to move back to Tennessee with us? Or you mean like a head doctor?

Counseling isn't a bad idea, and it could help you sort through all the pain. But I wasn't thinking of that exactly.

Then what?

Have you ever stopped to ask for God's help? Have you ever told Him you can't make it alone anymore?

How can I trust a God that took away my brother?

Listen to me. Almost two thousand years ago God let His own Son be taken away. He let people spit on Him, mock Him, beat Him, and kill Him on a crude wooden cross. In John's Gospel it says His Son was even stabbed . . . stabbed by a soldier's sword. God let it all happen and He did it for love, Benny. He did it for Mitch . . . you . . . me. He did it for love.

But why Mitch? Why my only brother?

I suspect that's something you'll never find out. I know it's hard, but you've got to stop asking why. It'll only tear you up more.

How can I? How can I stop?

Benny, there's not a single pain you're feeling that God didn't have when it came to giving up His only Son. Maybe leaving the questions with the Father is a place for you to begin.

It's so rough to . . . to want to go on.

Sure it's rough, but what else are you going to do? How else can you get on with your life?

You didn't know Mitch. You can't understand what he meant to me.

I'm no psychologist. I don't know the ins and outs of mourning, or anger, or coping with drugs in a family situation. You've got so many complex things to deal with, and I didn't mean to imply it's going to be a snap to work everything through, with or without a counselor. I only mean to say that it might be easier to let God take some of your load and walk through these days and weeks with you.

You almost make me want to believe.

That's good I suppose, but you're awfully confused right now. You need time to sort through what we've said. Benny, have you ever shared these things with anyone before?

I . . . I tried to.

Benny, you're such a good kid. I'm so glad I had you last year. You have depth—know what that means?

I've got a long way to go?

No, no. It doesn't mean that. It means you're very sensitive. You see things and you feel things deeply. We need men like that. We need strong men sensitive enough to care. Men who are tough and tender at the same time.

You think I could ever be like that?

Benny, I think you're already like that. You aren't feeling strong and tough right now, but you're still standing. After all this, you're still standing.

Feels like I'm barely cutting it.

Do you know how many boys I've taught who could go through what you have and survive? Maybe two. Maybe three. A lot of kids your age have never learned to cope . . . they've never had to. You've been coping all your life. That has to count for something.

You make it sound like there's good in all this. Like I'm special.

Oh, you are. You are. And I think your background can give you a depth and maturity years ahead of your time. As difficult as it is to see now, value can come from these hurts of yours.

How though?

It's too soon to tell. But there's another verse back here in Romans. Listen to it. It reads, "And we know that God causes all things to work together for good to those who love God, to those who are called according to his purpose." I don't know anyone else who could promise that.

I still don't see how any of this can amount to good.

I don't think God ever wants tragedies and pain. But the good thing with Him is that He can make it count for something. He can bring hope to something utterly hopeless. You can't take that verse I just read all alone, Benny. Keep in mind that some—and only some, not all—some things won't be clearly seen until Heaven. Still there's a whole lot of good that God can resurrect from your upbringing. Things that you can see and touch right in this lifetime.

I never once felt there was any hope for me. Hope was always for the smart kids. The rich kids. The kids with storybook families.

When we come to know our Father, when we give our lives to Him, He brings in a wealth of hope. Not hope in our abilities, but hope in what He can do.

I feel like I've been through World War III tonight. And still it's like a weight's off my chest. Like I can even breathe in deep again.

Benny, don't keep things bottled up inside. When you get back to Tennessee next week, look around for someone you can trust. A counselor. A minister. A youth leader. A teacher. I don't know, just find someone. Someone you can go to who will help you unload all these built-up emotions.

There's a counselor at school. I think he really cares. He even came to Mitch's funeral.

Then start with him. Let him help you.

I can't tell you how much better I feel.

And that makes me feel good too.

Is that clock right?

I think so.

My cousin's going to have a heart attack!

I'm sorry you've got to go. I'll get your jacket.

I promised his car back by 11:00 and there's no way I'll make it now. Didn't think I'd be here this long!

Want to use my phone?

No, it's more fun to make him sweat it out!

Benny!

Just teasing. It'll be okay. He's a good waiter.

Will you come back and see me again? It doesn't have to be this week, but when you visit your cousin again?

You know I will.

And since you've gone to all that trouble to get my phone number . . . well, if you're ever in a jam and there's no one to talk to . . . use it.

Where do you want me to put my glass and this Pepsi bottle?

Leave them right there. I'll straighten up in the morning.

I don't know what to say. It may be a while till I see you next.

Can I give you something?

Like what?

Here, take this with you. Read it. Think about it.

But it's your Bible. I can't take your Bible.

You think I only keep one of these around? Now here—go on and take it.

Miss Campbell.

Benny.

Okay. And you know I'll take good care of it.

Just read it!

You're sounding more and more like that teacher I remember.

I'll take that as a compliment, young man.

Do. It is.

Here, let me get that latch. It sticks all the time. I'd hate to leave by this door in a fire, know what I mean?

Miss Campbell, thanks.

Benny, you're okay. You're going to make it.

See ya. Go with God and all that stuff.

You, too, Benny. Go with God. And . . . and be careful.

Father, Benny hurts. He grieves. He's got so much to cope with. Keep Your hand on him. Protect him. Let him know Your love. Amen.

10

The Pearl

"Sorry, but it's regulations. I can't let you see her until you've been checked," the guard said while rattling a fistful of keys on a huge silver ring.

"Oh," I answered and clutched the leather strap on my purse for some immediate sense of security.

"Have a seat. Did you bring anything for her? Anything at all?" The plastic identification card clipped to the attendant's pocket bore her picture and the name Grettle W. Eaton. She was a middle-aged woman whose dark navy uniform made her look attractive and even sophisticated.

"Only a letter," I replied. "It's from one of her school friends and I told her I'd hand deliver it to Pearl."

"Mail has to be cleared," the woman in blue replied.

I fumbled through my purse and produced the pink envelope. "Here it is. I'm sure there's nothing offensive in it."

"Your little friend even put a stamp on it?" she mused.

"I don't follow what you mean."

"We always look at the stamps first. A couple times a month we get stamps with cocaine, heroine, or even a small acid tablet crushed underneath."

She cautiously lifted a corner of the stamp, pulled it back and continued, "The sender usually licks around the outer edges and hides the drug in the center. See? This one's clean."

I gulped and offered the only answer I knew to give, "I see."

"Just to be sure, I need to look inside. Most people think we open letters to read them, but the truth is we're inspecting the mail for thin and sharp things like razor blades. They get passed a lot. And drugs. We've even found a few letters that were previously soaked in a drug solution and dried. The juvenile who receives it will chew and chew the paper to get a quick high. So, naturally, we're forced to be careful."

I watched as she held the stationery up to the light and rubbed the pages against each other. After a moment's examination she handed both letter and envelope back to me. "This is okay. I'm sure of it. Did you bring anything else for her?"

"No," I replied. "Thought I'd see what she needed or wanted first. I hope to be back early next week."

"Let me call upstairs for her now," the receiving attendant said, and wheeled around in her chair to reach the telephone. She dialed three digits and paused a moment. "Lucy, this is Grettle in 2-W. We're ready for Pearl Lloyds as soon as you can arrange to bring her down. No, it's an old teacher of hers. Actually," Grettle stopped and glanced at me, "she's not that old!"

I smiled back, somewhat embarrassed at bringing only twenty-five years of life and experience to the situation.

"Lucy?" Grettle continued, "put her classification down as a helping professional under section five. She got clearance yesterday through Mr. Ransburgh himself. Ten minutes? See you then."

Grettle slid the phone back in its place and spoke, "You've got to leave everything with me. Your handbag. Jewelry. Anything in your pockets. It's all got to stay behind."

I set my purse squarely on the table and stood up to check the pockets in my jeans. I purposefully turned them inside-out just so she could see. "Nothing in them but my car keys," I said.

"You'll have to leave them too. We had a case last winter where someone slipped a house key to a young suicidal. That's all it took."

"Brother," I said aloud and stuffed my keys, watch, and rings into the large brown envelope Grettle provided. "How do you cope with all this?"

"I know it sounds crazy, but you get used to it. When my shift is over and it's time to go, I've learned to leave everything at work. It's the only way."

"Don't you ever feel overwhelmed with the hurt you see?"

"Oh, I don't know if I'd say overwhelmed. I get sad sometimes. Like with the one you're here to visit. Pearl Lloyds. Now she's a pathetic kid."

"How do you mean?" I asked.

"I worked on her floor all last week. She hardly eats. She hasn't opened up yet, not even with our staff psychologist or the counselor who's been assigned her case. She won't take advantage of the free time in the lounge each afternoon, which is something *all* kids do when they're in lockup. Pearl's not angry with us. She's not rebellious. She doesn't even begin to fit the hardcore stereotype we generally get. The only·reason she's in confinement is because of her threats to run away again."

I sat back down and crossed my legs. "I . . . I heard the State Highway Patrol picked her up about five hundred miles west of here the last time she took off. It's hard to believe she's the same contented girl I knew at school. I bet Pearl stopped by my room every other day to talk before she left for home. I enjoyed her so much. She was one of my top students."

"It's my guess," Grettle said, "she probably needs you right now. Someone she knows. Someone she likes and trusts. I hope you can penetrate that silence of hers."

"Did you tell her I was coming today?" I asked.

"No. Some people set up appointments and never show. Then the kids either get more depressed or more hostile. It's pretty sticky for us to handle."

"Has her family been in?"

"Not that I know of. The courts assigned Pearl here three weeks ago and I'm pretty sure you're the only one who's come. If I remember correctly, the other count brought against her was unruly conduct. Her mother's the one who pressed for legal action, so it doesn't surprise me the family's kept its distance. Probably best for a while."

"There are just so many things that don't add up," I responded. "It's true I've never had to live with my kids in their homes, but I can usually spot the ones who'd be awful to manage. Pearl is definitely *not* one of them. She's got a big and gentle heart; at least she did have two months ago when school let out."

With that Grettle got up, walked over to a nearby metal door and peered through its glass window. She waved hello to someone inside. Then she turned toward me, "Lucy just brought her in and sat her down on this side of the table. You ready to try?"

"I think so. Will you be in there with us?" I asked.

"No, Lucy will. Actually, she'll be right outside the glass partition in case you need anything. Because of your visiting status I doubt if she'll even get involved. You'll see what I mean when you go in."

"Fine," I answered and made my way over to the entrance door.

"Take as long as you want. When you want to come back out, press the red button by the door, wait ten seconds, and then turn the handle. This one's on a special circuit system."

I wiped my palms against my jeans. "I . . . I think I'm ready now."

"Wait here until I go back to my desk and unlock the door. Push it open when you hear the ringing sound. Good luck," Grettle said and walked away.

The electric buzzing was more like a steel *pop* and I knew I must push the cold metal door and push it now. My heart was pounding hard. "Dear God," I whispered, "give me the strength, words, and compassion Pearl needs. Help me through this. I'm scared." With nothing left to do, I breathed deeply and moved forward.

Pearl's head was slumped face down on the small wooden table top. Both of her arms protectively buried it there. As I brushed by Pearl I acknowledged the observing attendant through the glass wall and then pulled out the padded chair opposite my tired friend. I intentionally made noise sitting down by clearing my throat. Still, young Pearl did not move.

"My, my, my," I said jokingly. "You'd think I was going to lecture you on Emerson, Thoreau, or—perish forbid—Shakespeare himself, the way you're already tuned out to nap."

No response.

"And to think I came all this distance, got lost twice, just to hear my own voice."

Slowly Pearl's arms straightened out and she raised her head from the table. She squinted temporarily from the sudden glare of light, then opened her eyes in disbelief. "Miss Campbell, it *is* you!" I couldn't tell if there was more excitement in her voice or trembling fear.

Within seconds I reached out and cupped her wrist in my left hand. "Pearl, Pearl! I was so worried about you!"

Her eyes filled up with tears and she squeezed my arm hard. "Miss Campbell, I don't believe you came. It's just I figured I'd never see you again."

"How could I *not* come when I learned you were here?" I said.

"But when did you find out? How?"

"Last weekend through Marty. She dropped by your house and telephoned me afterwards. Then Monday and Tuesday I made a half dozen calls and, well, here I am. This isn't exactly the easiest place to get into, you know."

"Or to get out of," Pearl groaned. "Was Marty upset?"

"Of course she was. That reminds me—she gave me a letter for you and I left it outside by my purse. I'll have to get it to you later."

Pearl jerked her hands from the table to wipe away the tears and fumble awkwardly with her dark brown hair. "I must look awful. My face. My hair like this. These clothes. I must look awful."

We both knew she spoke the painful truth.

"Why, Pearl Marcia Lloyds, I am ashamed of you!" I raved with intentionally wide and exaggerated gestures. "I put on my very best summer T-shirt, my pressed jeans, not to mention my finest Converse All Star racers. *And to think I find you like this?*"

We enjoyed a hearty laugh.

"You haven't changed," Pearl admitted. "Hey, you didn't cut your hair, did you?" she asked as an afterthought.

"No, no. It's all here," I answered and pulled out the wooden peg which kept the hair knot loosely in place. "There, you see? What a mess when I drive with the windows down. It blows all around and gets caught on the steering wheel, the shoulder strap, my glasses, you name it!"

"You wanna know what I think?" Pearl grinned from ear to ear. "I think it must be the speed you travel!"

"Funny, funny," I chuckled and raised a finger. "That's one for you."

In the moment of silence which followed we both grew serious and groped for words. It was Pearl who began. "I can't tell you, Miss Campbell, how good it is to see you."

"Same here for me too," I said. "But Pearl? Pearl, what's happened since I saw you last?"

"You mean how did I get here?"

I raised my eyebrows and nodded yes.

She managed a wobbly smile. "I guess some judge decided to throw the book at me."

"You're avoiding my question," I interjected.

"I know, I know. It just got so bad I couldn't take it at home anymore. I left, Miss Campbell. It's that simple."

I folded my hands on the desk top. "Couldn't you and your parents work out your differences? They both seemed like nice, reasonable people when I met them at the choir concert. Was running away your only alternative?"

"I tell you I couldn't take it anymore," she responded in earnest. "My mother . . . and Dirk, my stepfather . . . we were always into it. I had to get away from town." Pearl's lip started to quiver, and I again saw her eyes get watery and red.

"Where did you end up going, Pearl? How did you survive on the road?"

"Oh, I don't know," she whispered and looked down at her lap. "The first time I went north. Walked along the highway and thumbed rides."

"Didn't you take anything with you?"

"Only the clothes on my back. That's all. Except the first time I took $20.00 from my mother's purse. That didn't go too far."

"Weren't you scared?"

"Suppose so, but nothing like this last time out west. Half a dozen times I went into stores and stole food under my shirt. One guy caught me red-handed and I flew out when he turned around to call the cops. You talk about scared, I was scared all right. I slept in an alley behind trash cans four or five nights. You bet I was scared, Miss Campbell, and you'd probably desert me if I told you the rest of it."

"That's not so, Pearl," I said gently. "You ought to know by now I care a lot about you. I'll accept you no matter what."

She brought her hands up to shield her eyes and face from me. There was a long pause and then Pearl confided, "I . . . I didn't have any money. *I was hungry.* I . . . I picked up a guy for a lousy meal. Some other guys for a place to stay. I hate myself and I guess I deserve to be here."

"You and I," I said, "we've had many talks, haven't we?"

"Uh-huh," Pearl sniffled from behind protective hands.

"And we've always tried to be honest, right?"

"I think so."

"Even when it was painful?" I asked.

"Yes, yes, even then."

"Pearl, I know there's something more. Deep down inside I know there's something else at the root of all this."

Suddenly Pearl pulled away from the table and stood. She walked around the small conference room, stopped by the only window and gazed outside. I checked for a positive response from Lucy, the waiting attendant, then arose from my chair and went beside Pearl.

"The grass . . . the trees . . . it's all so peaceful out there," Pearl uttered and placed her elbows against the ledge. She leaned forward into the small recess.

"Yes it is," I commented.

"So peaceful," she repeated a second time softly. "Seems like months since I was outside."

"Pearl? Pearl, they tell me you don't eat much. They tell me you hardly communicate unless it's to make another threat to run. Your probation officer told me you literally blew up in court, almost like you wanted to be put away somewhere. That is, anywhere away from home. He said even with the previous record of your journey up north, the judge was willing to give you another chance until you got mighty arrogant.

"Pearl, why would you prefer stealing from strangers to being with your family? Why would you sell yourself for a place to stay in distant cities when you have a home of your own? What could be that awful to drive you away?"

"I wish my father was here," she said.

"I do too, but you know that's impossible. Your father's gone, Pearl. He died years ago in that car crash. Please don't tear yourself up by hoping for something that just can't be."

"He gave me a stuffed panda bear a few days before his accident. It's blue and I used to hug and hug and hug it. I named him Puddles. About three years ago I lost one of his coal black eyes. I looked everywhere, but I never did find it. I miss Puddles. I miss my father."

"Please, Pearl. I don't want to badger you, but I'm going to ask you point-blank. What was so awful at home?"

"I hate him," she answered with growing contempt. "I hate my stepfather. He's not my real dad and I just hate him."

"When did all this start?" I wondered aloud, trying to piece together the fragments of her puzzle. "How many times did you mention Dirk after school to me, and never once did I detect feelings of hatred. Indifference maybe, but never hatred."

"I would *die* before I go back there. I . . . I just keep seeing him," she sighed deeply. "That's why I can't sleep. That's why I keep running."

"Pearl, please look at me. Please turn around. Please?" I placed my hand firmly on her shoulder and kept it there. Eventually she straightened up from the window and turned toward me. Her face was downcast and her eyes were shut.

I touched my other hand to her chin. "You can look at me because I'm going to accept you. I'm not going to run out and leave you. Please trust me. I want to help."

"You probably won't believe me, either," Pearl said and tensed the muscles in her body. "I tried to tell my mom, and she wouldn't believe me."

"Wouldn't believe *what*, Pearl?"

"I can't say the words, Miss Campbell. I'm too ashamed." Her eyes were still closed, but now there were teardrops running down her pale cheeks.

At first the only suspicion I had seemed remote. But as I silently watched the salty hot tears drip from Pearl's chin onto my hand, I realized I must ask to be sure. I must ask to know beyond all doubt. "Pearl, your stepfather," I whispered. *"Pearl, did he rape you?"*

Her countenance conveyed more than inner hurt. It conveyed terror, and in an instant she began to weep uncontrollably. I took the one step between us and drew her close. She thrust her face into my shoulder and flung her shaking, tight arms around me. The truth was now tragically obvious: Pearl Marcia Lloyds had indeed been raped.

"Dear God," I confessed in amazement. "That's what this is

all about. Now I understand. I understand completely."

For what seemed like an eternity I sheltered my trembling, frightened Pearl and prayed for her. What a burden she had borne all this time. What a price she had paid for the hideous act upon her. No wonder she was not the same optimistic girl I had left behind only a few short months ago. Much too much had happened in her world since then.

As I groped for the right words to calm and comfort, my thoughts were interrupted by a foreign voice. "I can take over now," Lucy spoke above Pearl's hysterical cries. In the confusion I had failed to see the observing attendant make her way toward us.

"Please, Ma'am," I urged. Tears were in my own eyes too, and I shook my head back and forth to signify my desire to hold Pearl. "Please?"

Lucy did not answer, but squeezed my arm in agreement. She then pulled out a box of tissues, set it on the table top and made her way back to the observing booth.

"It's okay," I said and rocked Pearl gently. "Shhh. Try to relax."

"No, not once," Pearl wailed, "but again and again and again. He bought a gun and said if I didn't go along, he'd use it on Christy. She's only four years old. Why would he do that? Why? Why?"

"Shhh, Pearl," I said while my own tears rolled onto her lifeless hair. "Relax. You're here with me now. You're safe. Hold on to me, Pearl. Hold on."

"It started just after school. He came to me when Mom was at work. She was always at work. And . . . and . . . the first time he said he had to teach me something. Later I ran out. I kept running and running and—"

"Shhh. Come on, Pearl. You're shaking. Relax now. Try to relax."

"I just couldn't stay," she wept. "Not after all those times he came to me late. I'm so awful and I hate him. They kept bringing me back home. It would start all over again. And I had to go. I had to."

I clutched her more tightly. "Pearl, you're here now. You aren't at home. Do you understand? You're safe now. Shhh, just relax. Pearl, relax."

"But . . . but he was going to kill Christy. I saw the gun. He made me touch it. He . . . he . . . he. . . ."

"Shhh, relax. Relax. That's it, Pearl. Just relax. Shhh."

If confession is good for the soul, then young Pearl began the long journey back to wholeness that summer day of my first visit. Never before in my role as teacher had I encountered the emotional intensity and exhaustion like those hours when I upheld my tired and weary friend. For Pearl and me, that experience cemented us to each other in a strong bond of love that would not—indeed *could not*—be shaken. Not even with the greater test of time and further miles of distance.

For the record I feel I must point out that our relationship did not begin in the detention conference room on a hot summer morning. Far from it. Just as surely as one snowflake falling upon another makes in time a blanket of white, so our previous talks (many as they were) steadily produced the tempered, receptive soil for deep trust. It could not have happened any other way.

Pearl's life today is far from being healed, but once the truth was exposed there came many changes in and around her. After several legal hearings and time in jail, the courts eventually released the stepfather with the condition he seek and maintain psychiatric help. And Pearl? Her eating and sleeping habits improved immediately after her first day of disclosure. Within the month she was transferred to a freer youth center where she continued extensive counseling. Although her mother and stepfather divorced a year later, Pearl preferred to live in holding facilities and youth homes across the state rather than reunite with what was left of her family. Her circle of trust was so grossly broken I seriously doubt if she will ever choose to return.

Today the two of us keep in touch, and I see her when I can. There are times we continue to enjoy the tingle of laughter. And there are times we find for crying. Especially when we exchange hugs, gifts, or have to say good-bye. Parting is always hard for both of us.

Deep scars that plunge our most intimate selves do not easily heal. Nor do they magically go away. I believe something of Pearl's anguish will be with her until the day she dies. I hope and pray she will have learned to cope long before then, but the seed of contamination she experienced at home and on the road will take its toll somehow. Sadly there are thousands of women like her who will attest to that.

Still, despite the pain and long process of reconstruction, there is hope for a full and meaningful life. I have had many opportunities in person, by letter or phone to share my faith with Pearl. Caring enough to listen and work with her through her struggles has won me center stage to say what I want and be heard. I've seen the resistance and bitterness against God diminish to childlike openness and honest searching. For the first time in her life, Pearl attends a church when it's possible, and she reads a Bible I gave her for daily nurturing. It comforts me deep inside to know that Pearl Lloyds is not far from the kingdom of God.

I have never met a braver youth, and I thank the Father for bringing Pearl into my classroom and into my life. As I remind her often, the oyster's rough irritating grain of sand, encased by years of cultivation, someday becomes a smooth and lustrous gem. This tragic intrusion into Pearl's life can be molded and shaped into a valued treasure. I do not know how and I do not know when, but with the Father's touch, it has to. She is His living Pearl of great worth.

Lord, how hard it is to see You as Father when our earthly relationships can disgrace the very name by which You are called. Show us what You are really like. Even today bring hope, love, and inner healing. Amen.

11

Jonas and the Great Church Debate

Through the windshield I saw the weather sign across the street blink 85 degrees, and it was a scorcher of a Saturday to sit in the hot, hot car. The temperature gauge had already inched its way over to "H" in the ten minutes I had waited, and there were still four more automobiles bumper to bumper ahead. "What lousy timing," I thought. "I should have done this last week instead of waiting until the last minute."

By the time I pulled between the fluorescent markers I was eager to jump out of the car. "I've got a free coupon," I told the man in cutoffs. "It expires today."

"Fine, fine," he replied and thumped his hand on the roof of my car. "We'll give this little baby the best interior and exterior car wash it's ever had in only twelve minutes."

I tossed my keys to him and went inside the waiting area to find relief from the humid heat. Luckily there was a bottled water machine there. I pulled out a Dixie cup from the dispenser and refilled it twice. Ah, water! It was when I crushed the paper cup flat and threw it inside the trash can that I faintly heard my name. I glanced to my right and left, yet I was alone except for an elderly gentleman I did not know. Again I heard my name, but this time it was accompanied by tapping sounds on the glass window behind me. I whirled around to find a tall and bronze young man on the opposite side, waving his soapy arms.

"Hi, Jonas! Hi!" I shouted.

For several minutes we did our best at charading messages through the transparent barrier: *How are you? Do you still teach? You have a nice car. Isn't it hot? How long have you worked here?* Finally Jonas threw up his hands (pantomiming and such were not always my strength, either) and disappeared from his catwalk through a maze of huge washing brushes. Miraculously within sixty seconds he was standing beside me in nothing but gym trunks and tennis shoes. Jonas was, for the most part, dripping wet.

"You mean they trust kids like you with peoples' cars?" I teased. "I should have left my hubcaps at home today!"

"Listen here, Miss C. You'll be lucky to leave with your tires knowing the crew I left outside. I'm the only one holding them back. When I saw the parking sticker in your front window, I knew I had to check out who was here from school. You just better appreciate me." He flashed a big smile and scratched his tanned chest.

"Oh, I do. Honest I do. Jonas, you're looking more handsome than ever. I bet that curly black mustache makes you a big hit with the ladies, huh?"

Jonas stretched his arms out wide and closed his eyes. "When you've got it, *you've got it!*"

"Good grief," I answered. "Whatever happened to the bold and aggressive kid I remember from class a year or so ago? Have you been taking lessons in modesty or something?"

"I was just telling you the truth," he said. "Listen, I got to get back out there, but I'm through in half an hour. You had lunch yet?"

"No. What did you have in mind?" I replied.

Jonas shifted his weight from foot to foot. He was trying to hurry. "Why don't you go across to Artie's Diner and I'll meet you? Now that I have a job I can even pick up the tab."

"Is there something you wanted to discuss?" I asked.

"Sort of. I'd just like to talk. Nothing big."

I paused for a moment and looked for sincerity in his expression. "Okay. Half an hour it is. I'll go on over when my car's done."

"See you later," he said and jogged away.

"Oh, Jonas? Jonas?" I shouted above the noise of machinery. "Do you think you can locate a T-shirt?"

"Gottcha, Miss C.," he yelled and darted out of sight.

I sipped ice tea as I enjoyed the air conditioned atmosphere of the restaurant. When my drink was finished I passed the time by pinching out small bits of the styrofoam cup along the brim with my finger and thumb. Round and round I turned the ever shrinking cup and threw the growing clutter of pieces inside it.

"Miss C.?" I heard over my shoulder as Jonas inspected my handiwork.

"Jonas! Sit down. Sit down."

He slid into his side of the booth. "I said your name twice. What on earth are you doing?"

"Some people pluck daisy petals," I answered philosophically. "I've got this thing for styrofoam cups. You see, it puts me in tune with the universe and six other planets!"

"Oh, yeah? Sounds pretty spooky to me. But if you want to know the truth, I like to bite mine and make little teeth marks all around the top edge. I've got it down to a science."

"And you thought *I was crazy*? Let's order!"

My tuna fish sandwich and salad came rather quickly, but it took longer for Jonas' Big Buster Burger, double order of fries and Mighty Man Shake. While we ate we updated each other on students and teachers we both knew in common, we rehashed several of the old projects Jonas had done in my class, and we discussed changes brought about by national current events. Then the dialogue swung back to us.

"Yeah, I remember all sorts of things about you," Jonas boasted. "Things besides what you taught, I mean."

"Like what?" I challenged and took the last bite of my sandwich.

"You love Chinese food best of all, you have a big fancy stereo system and you play pretty good tennis."

"How do you know all that?" I asked.

"Well, you told us in class one time about the food. I remember because all of us went BLAH! when you said it was Chinese. The stereo set? I overheard you ask Mr. Jenkins one time about an imported tape deck you were adding onto your system. Pretty expensive stuff if you ask me. And the tennis bit? I watched you play one afternoon on the courts behind the school. I think it was you and Miss Huntly. You didn't see me because I was inside the cafeteria serving a detention, but I know it was you. You had one of those new steel rackets."

"Goodness, I've got to be more careful," I answered back. "There are little eyes and ears everywhere!"

Jonas vacuumed the final drops of his Mighty Man Shake through the red and white straw and then said, "I know this is kind of out in left field, but I've wanted to ask you something ever since I sat down."

I took another drink of water. "Ask. Go ahead."

He pointed in the direction of the salt and pepper shakers. "What in the world is that leather thing on your key chain there?"

"Oh, this?" I said and picked up my keys from off the table. "It's a fish."

"I *know* it's a fish, but what's that inside the outline?"

"First, it's called an ichthus. Those are Greek letters burned into the leather. Here, look at it more closely."

He took the key ring from my hand. "But what do they mean?"

"The fish is really a symbol. Early Christians used to put it on their doorposts, in the sand, or wherever. It was like a secret code of trust from one believer to another. Most people think the cross was the first symbol of Christianity, but they're mistaken. It was the fish."

"Don't tell me you're a religious fanatic," he scoffed and plunked the keys into my palm.

"What do you mean?" I asked.

For the first time in our conversation Jonas seemed troubled and preoccupied. "My mother—she's one. That's kind of what I wanted to talk to you about." He stopped a moment and pushed aside his plate and napkin. "You remember my folks were split up? I'm the only kid left at home now, and, well, I wanted to go with my father but he said no. He moved a couple years ago and married some lady who has a ton of little kids. I wanted to go with him because I could hardly understand my mother anymore. In fact—please don't hate me—I quit school six months ago just after I turned sixteen. I left home for a while and bummed around. Then I got tired and came back."

"Jonas, I didn't know about your quitting school. I'm sorry to hear that. Once a person quits, it's hard to go back."

"Well, it seemed like a waste of time. Besides, I wanted to make some money and kind of get my head together. But this business with my mother is driving me crazy."

"How is she a fanatic, Jonas? What do you mean?"

"Here goes," he answered and took a deep breath. "Better let me get comfortable first. We may be here all afternoon."

Jonas swung around sideways in the booth so that his back leaned against the wall and his feet hung over the edge of the seat. He perched one elbow on the table and dropped the other arm into his lap. "Well, for starters," he said, "Mom's usually at her church about four nights a week. She started going there right before the divorce was final. I like loud music, Miss C., but that place puts rock concerts to shame. And I'm not exaggerating, either: I can't even hear myself *think* when I'm there. Her minister is something else. He's always going back and forth on stage yelling at the top of his lungs. Why does he have to yell to be heard? Why can't he talk in a normal tone of voice? If he isn't shouting at us, he's weeping. In fact it's usually both at the same time, now that I think about it.

"He talks about how clean his mother's floor was, how our country is going down a chute straight to Hell, how his daddy—he still calls him daddy—used to make him toe the line. And then he gets on these healing speeches. He says things like, 'If you're sick, you deserve to be sick. Just cast Satan away! You have the power if you want to use it. You disgrace God every time you have a headache because you've let Satan come into your mind and body.'

"I tell my mother I don't want any part of it. The only reason I even went was simply to be with her since she's hardly ever home. I mean the services can go on until midnight, Miss C. Really. And then the nights she's not at church, she'll find some guy on TV just like her minister. Even Jeffrey, the guy who's moved in with Mom, is getting tired of it."

"This Jeffrey," I interrupted. "You mean he rents at your house?"

"No, my mom and him got this thing going. He's been living with us for over a year. I resent him being there, and they argue every other day now. He says she hardly spends any time with him. Well have I got news for him—she's my mother and she NEVER spends time with me! And still they call themselves born again, baptized in the Spirit, Christians. It's just something else I don't understand."

Jonas ran his hand through his hair and continued. "You know, some nights when Mom and him were both out, I'd turn on that religious station and watch it by myself. I—I wanted to believe, and I tried to keep an open mind, but it's like every show has its own gimmick. On one it's thinking on the positive side for everything you want to be or do, and that's all the minister talks about. He sounds more like a businessman than anything else. I don't think I've ever heard him preach straight from the Bible. Even I know a sermon should come from the Bible.

"Another show is stuck on the God and country idea with flags on the lapel and Bibles in hand. And one is all miracles and healing. Some are loud music, loud preaching, loud everything. To me they all seem like gimmicks. Kind of like hooks to get people to bite.

"The other night I sat through a Christain talk show just out of curiosity. Miss C., I clocked fifteen minutes out of every thirty that the host asked for money to help him stay on the air. He said every financial gift to his ministry was a way to defeat the devil. Can you believe that? It's like a vicious circle: *give us more money so we can get more time to ask for more money.*

"The way it looks to me, if it's not dollar talk on all these shows, then it's *write us! Or call us at the number in front of you! Or send in for offer #5063!* You know, for a special plaque, pin, record, book, bumper sticker, genuine copy of this or that. After all, how else can every religious TV show aim to make it around the world?

"Miss C., you and I both know they have to be bringing in millions of dollars. Makes me want to buy a three piece suit, grab a microphone, and hop right on the TV bandwagon myself. I'm not religious and I don't pretend to be, but I can't see Jesus pulling this kind of stuff. Can you?"

I debated in silence for a moment on how to handle the situation. How could I explain the television phenomenon and the differences in beliefs and practices when I struggled with some of the same questions myself? "Jonas, I honestly don't know how to respond or where to begin to sort everything out for you. You've hit on some very touchy issues."

"Well, are you a fanatic like them?" he challenged.

"No, I'm not like them."

"Then what do you believe? Let's hear it," Jonas demanded.

When I quietly fumbled for the right approach he added, "Please?"

"Jonas," I began, "I understand why you're confused. Sometimes I am too. I've probably watched the very same programs you've seen, and I've gotten up and turned the channel when I'd reached a saturation point. I've wondered, like you, about their constant plea for finances. I've wondered about the little churches down the street and how they could possibly compete with the appeal of what I call the Video Church. I don't know if it's any comfort to you, but I think a lot of your observations contain an element of truth."

"But how, Miss C.? How do you make sense of it all? How can you know who to trust or what to believe?"

"When I get bombarded by sensational Christian books, speakers, or programs from the Video Church, I remember my old music teacher. If I got lazy with practice or in over my head during my lesson he'd always say, 'Jean, back to basics,' and he'd pull out my very first book. Then we'd review for a while. It got my attention back on the important things."

Jonas seemed desperate to understand. "I don't get the connection."

"Well, when I get confused—and I *do* get confused, Jonas—I just pray that God will take me back to basics. Back to himself, back to His love and forgiveness, back to His Son's sacrifice, back to quiet study of the Bible. Now I know there are TV ministers who preach they believe the Bible and nothing but the Bible. But frankly, Jonas," I said gently, "I'm concerned with some whose life-styles do not match their own noble words. I'm concerned over those who fail to preach with depth and scholarship. I confess I shy away if I see they're caught up in constant emotional fervor, technicolor visions, or quickie formulas on how to live the Christian life. Those kinds of speakers do not point me to the Father, Jonas. They point me to themselves."

I stopped to give Jonas an opportunity to react. Instead he urged, "Go on. I'm listening."

"I know there are some true and honest evangelists. I know that the Video Church has an appeal and reaches some people. So I can't, I simply can't discount everything. I just try not to wrestle with TV ministries too much. My strength has never come from there. At best, I think most religious programs offer only a portion of the total truth. A few of them may supplement a good steady diet of the local church, but they can never take its place. At least I don't think so."

"Wait a minute," Jonas interjected. "What do you mean by the local church?"

"I mean churches around where we live. Neighborhood and city churches. Churches with flesh and blood people who sit beside me, who listen as I listen, and who interact with me."

"Oh," he answered. "I get it now."

"Just like on TV, we can still get overwhelmed with the varieties of beliefs in the local churches too. You've got to remind yourself, though, that the church your mother attends is just one of a hundred churches in this city. Be careful not to generalize and assume they're all alike. Hers is only one, Jonas. Do you see?"

"Kind of," he said. "Remember when I told you I left home and bummed around?"

"Yes," I replied.

"Well, believe it or not, I stopped in at a couple churches. One was even more boring than school. Stand up, sit down. Stand up, sit down. It was definitely cold. You know, women in their basic mink stoles and all that? I left halfway through the service. I knew I didn't belong there.

"The other church seemed friendlier. At least the people smiled at me, shook my hand, and showed me a seat. Anyway, I stuck it out the whole hour and a half in that one. Why is it if both places worship the same God, they're so different? I don't mean just the looks of the church buildings, I mean in what they said and did in their services?"

I reached into my purse for a stick of gum, unwrapped it, and popped it in my mouth. Then I handed one across to Jonas and answered, "Over the past few years I've been at a number of places. I've spoken at many different churches. Even if I looked at two churches with the same name, I know I'd find differences. It gets a little confusing sometimes, but I think differences will always be with us.

"Don't get me wrong," I said and put out my hand. "I'm not saying it doesn't matter where you go. I think you need to visit around, Jonas, until you find a place where you feel comfortable with the people and with the way the Bible is interpreted as you study more of it yourself. If you find they compromise everything in Scripture or, on the other hand, have no tolerance for any differing opinions, then I'd say keep visiting.

"You know, Jonas, I'm sure it matters to God that we go to a church, and it matters to Him what that specific church is for us. But I think the most important issue at the heart of all this is what we do with Him in our day-to-day lives. We can attend the finest churches in the world and still walk away unfulfilled, unchanged, and a stranger to God. Churches can't offer a new life. Only God can.

"The important issue is have I given my life to God? Have I accepted His Son as my Savior? Have I asked for His forgiveness? Have I come face-to-face with His death, the empty tomb, and His promise for re-entry?

"Earlier I said that Christian television couldn't take the place of the local church. I believe that. Now I'm telling you the local church can't take the place of daily fellowship with God. That comes from time alone in prayer, in quietness, in reading from the Bible. These are of the utmost importance, and the church you choose should point you in this direction, Jonas."

"But what can I do about my mother and where she goes?" he asked.

"You're coping with two problems. Where your mother attends church is only one, and I don't know if you'll ever be able to do anything about that. She may go there the rest of her life, or she could change her mind next week. Who knows?

"Your second problem is a little more hopeful in terms of what you can do. I think you really need to sit down one-on-one with your mother and tell her how you feel. Have you ever tried a gentle, direct approach with her?"

I could see Jonas was embarrassed. "No, not exactly," he said, "I figured she wouldn't take me seriously."

"Don't you think if you told her how much you still need her, she'd listen? How many teens say that to their parents these days? And don't you think if you explained that you wanted her to spend more time with you, she'd understand? You're sixteen, the youngest in your family; surely she realizes you won't be at home much longer.

"I can't promise anything, and I can only hope that sharing together will draw you closer. It's my guess she needs you as much as you need her. Could be she goes to church four nights a week because she never felt there was a reason to stay home. Remember way back when you asked to go with your father? Well, maybe your mother's misunderstood that all this time. How could she not have felt rejected by your initial choice? Don't you think it's time she knows you loved her then and you love her now?"

Red flushed across his face, and he wore a boyish smile. "Yeah, you're right. Everything you've said has made sense. My mom—she's about the only family I have left. My two sisters live in other states. My dad's off in another life, and he doesn't need me. But my mom? She *does* mean a lot, if we could just work out a few things."

"Telling her you love her is a great way to get started, Jonas."

"Miss C., could I ask you a favor?" he stammered.

"Sure," I answered. "What is it?"

"Well, could you kind of remember me—and my mom—well, you know—over the next couple days?"

"Consider it done."

"Thanks," Jonas replied.

"Do you mind if I also throw in a few prayers about your schooling?" I asked.

"What do you mean?"

"Jonas, you've missed only one semester, and the new one starts at the end of next month. It wouldn't be hard for you to phase back in and graduate on time with the rest of your classmates if you take summer school next year. Your mind is just too valuable to waste."

"Please do. Pray, I mean. I sure will give it some thought."

"Well, young man," I stated. "Where do we go from here?"

"I guess back out into the heat. You can crawl into your nice clean car and head home. Me? I'm going to zip off this shirt as soon as I get outside—notice I put it on just for you—and take a walk. Think I'll go through the park and give some thought to this afternoon. I came *so close* to calling off work today. I'm really glad I went in now."

"And I came so close to throwing away that free coupon for a car wash. I can't even recall how I got it. I just knew it expired today, and I decided to go for a ride. I think we were both meant to get together. What do you say?"

"Yeah. Think so too."

"You come back and see me this fall at school, Jonas."

"Okay."

"And thanks for lunch. How I wish I'd brought my camera. Who would have believed it? Jonas Francesco treating a former teacher like this!"

"Oh, yeah? Well, don't go spreading it around. I still have my reputation to protect, you know!"

"Take care, Jonas."

"You take care, Miss C.," he said and stood. "It's time to go."

"Right," I answered, "Let's go."

Father, today it is not easy to sort through religions and churches to find You. Help Jonas in his search. Help his mother in hers. Get them safely over the hurdles ahead. Together. In Your Son's name. Amen.

12

Sleep

March 10. 6:15 A.M. Bedroom.

The music from the clock radio seemed unusually loud and fierce that morning. When I could no longer stand the sound of rapid notes, I half-turned in bed and reached for the off switch beside me. For five slow minutes the single thought to go round and round in my mind was the desperate need I had for more sleep. I was groggy and I was nauseated. How could I possibly function without more sleep?

I pulled the blankets closer and pondered the increasing number of accumulated sick days I had. Surely, since this would be my one and only miss for the whole school year, no one could argue I missed for every little reason. Plus the classroom tasks planned for that particular day could easily be managed by even the newest of substitutes. Yes, this was the day for personal restoration. I was convinced of it.

When my clock blinked a red 6:30, I snapped on my desk light and squinted for the list of important phone numbers. It was then that I experienced an overwhelming, gnawing sensation in the back of my mind: I ought to go to school despite my tired and sick feeling. "But God," I thought, "I'm strung out, I *need* rest." I walked back over and sat on the bed. "Father, I'm exhausted. I don't feel good, but if you want me to go today, I'll go. Just please use me in a special way. In fact, I'll be looking for chances to make a difference."

I crawled out of bed in slow motion (this time for good) and headed for the bathroom. I hardly ever had trouble waking up in the mornings, yet I knew enough to attempt the aged remedy of facial cold water splashes. It seemed like a torturous cure, but it was worth a try. At least once.

8:42 A.M. Study hall.

Carrie Sherburne stared into my eyes and whispered, "Everything all right with you, Campbell? You look a little green around the gills."

"I think I'm going to make it. I just need some sleep, that's all."

"You can take a break if you want. We don't both need to be here all the time to supervise. The kids are quiet and studying. Go on and take a rest," she insisted. "You've covered for me before."

I pulled my shoulder away from the blackboard where it rested. "If you're sure you don't mind," I answered. "I'll just walk down to the rest room and stop for a drink. I think the fresh air could perk me up."

Carrie pointed to the door. "Shoo! Go on and take your time."

I made my exit and wandered through the hallway maze. The girls' rest room appealed much more to me than the women's lounge two floors down simply because it was closer. Today even a staircase seemed mountainous.

I stopped to sip water from the drinking fountain and then turned the corner to find the rest room door. Halfway into its zigzag entrance I was met by Blythe Kui, a fourteen-year-old student of mine, who tried to rush by.

"Here, here, here," I said. "What's the hurry?"

"I got to get back," Blythe replied with a great deal of tension in her voice. Her eyes were red and swollen.

"Blythe, have you been crying?" I asked. "Let's go inside and you can rinse your face."

She turned around and led the way back into the rest room. I spoke again, "Something must be wrong. Can you talk about it?"

Blythe reached for a paper towel and submerged it in cold water. I could tell she was crying again when she leaned forward over the sink. "It doesn't have anything to do with school," she mumbled.

"Did something happen at home?" I wondered.

"Home? Yeah, you could say that."

"Blythe, if you want to talk, I can listen." I backed away from her and leaned against the far sink. I stared at the floor in quietness a minute, praying for the sensitive gift of discernment.

She began, "Late last night I was going through some attic boxes, looking for some oil paints my mom said she had up there from her college days. I . . . I came to this old chest of papers and I was curious about why it was hidden away." Blythe stopped talking and patted her face with a wet towel. She was crying harder now.

"And you found something that upset you?" I asked.

"*Boy, did I!*"

I waited and said nothing.

"Try an official Certificate of Adoption from the State of Arizona," she sobbed. "They didn't even have the decency to tell me."

I was moved by the painful expression on her face. Obviously Blythe's parents had never before discussed the matter with her. "Do your folks know that you found out?"

"Beats me," she answered and cupped strands of her long blond hair behind her ears. "I went straight to my room and stayed there. Didn't sleep a wink."

"Were you crying all night?"

"Most of it."

"And you didn't tell your mom and dad?"

"No. What's there to say? *Thanks for being so honest?* Or *hello, hello, whoever you are?*"

"Blythe, your parents care. I know they do. Your dad's so proud of you, your awards, your grade point average. He told me once how much of a personal joy you've been to him. And your mother said the same thing. I think both of them would want to be with you now. You need to hear them out before you jump to any conclusions about them and about yourself."

She stopped crying and looked at me. "You aren't going to call them, are you?"

"No, I won't unless you want me to. But Blythe, you look beat. Maybe school isn't the best place for you right now."

"Where else can I go?"

"Why don't you go down to Guidance and ask to go home? Maybe talk it out with your parents and try to get some rest. I think you need to be at home."

She studied herself in the large wall mirror. "I sure don't want anybody to see me like this."

"Blythe, there's no reason your friends have to see you. We're in the middle of second period, right? Whose class are you supposed to be in?"

"History with Canfield."

"How does this sound? I could talk with Mrs. Canfield a second, get your books and walk you downstairs. Blythe, you need time with your family. Time alone."

"I sure don't want to stick around here," she whispered and blew her nose. "Do you think they'll let me go home?"

"I can't see how it would be a problem under the circumstances."

"Do you . . . do you think they'll let you call my mom to come get me? Maybe you could explain a little of it to her so she'd understand and not get mad. I don't want anyone else to know."

"Let's go down and see," I said. "You want to give it a try?"

"I . . . I guess so."

"And will you keep me posted on how things turn out? I care about you and your family."

Blythe turned and took three steps toward the doorway. "I know you do," she answered. "Thanks."

12:00 P.M. Cafeteria.

Carrie caught my attention and pulled out the empty seat beside her. "You're looking better," she said. "How's everything going?"

I filled the space to her left and popped off the lid to my yogurt container. "I feel more alert. There's nothing like my morning classes to wake me up."

Carrie bit into her yellow apple. "How'd it go with Blythe after your call?"

"The first thing Mrs. Kui did when she got here was to hug her. Blythe hugged her back and started to cry. It's kind of a personal matter between them, but I really believe they'll work it through. I'm glad I came today for no other reason than to have been here with Blythe. Makes me feel good that she trusts me and that we'll be closer because of this."

"What's it all about? A divorce situation in the home or what?"

"Carrie, Blythe asked me not to say anything and I promised to keep it quiet. I wouldn't feel right repeating it."

"Okay, I understand," she answered. "By the way, don't you ever get tired of raspberry yogurt?"

I finished stirring and raised a purplish spoonful. "Here. You want a taste to see what you've been missing?"

"Not on your life!" she issued in disgust. "Look—here comes Jack. Maybe you can give him some."

Jack sat directly across from us at our teachers' table. "Did I hear my name?" he asked. "Hope it wasn't said in vain."

"Not this time, Jack. Carrie just wanted you to try my yogurt."

"Yogurt? *I love yogurt!* It's good protein when you're exercising, jogging, working out. It's terrific."

"Well, you can have it," Carrie scowled.

"How's it going with you, Jack?" I asked. "I hardly see you. What are you doing these days in your English classes? You have three of them, don't you? And three math?"

"Right," he answered and grabbed for the catsup. "I'm trying to get my kids into poetry. Some classical material. We got sidetracked today on the Book of Psalms from the Bible, of all things. Greek mythology I can handle, but I'm really not too familiar with Psalms. Aren't there close to a hundred poems in the collection?"

"A hundred and fifty," I replied.

"We never covered that stuff in college. They should have required us to read some Bible literature, but they didn't. Perhaps it was because of my double major or something."

"Jack, can I offer a suggestion?" I asked and breathed a prayer for an open door.

"Sure, go ahead."

"We keep hearing about team teaching at every other faculty meeting, and both poetry and Bible literature are personal favorites of mine. What would you think if I worked up a session on the poetical contents in Psalms and presented it to your classes?"

"Like how? I'm wide open for any change of pace."

"I could give them an historical overview of the book as well as some facts about its authors. Then I could discuss the usual terminology like simile, metaphor, personification, hyperbole, and so on, but give examples right from Psalms on the overhead. We could point out the different themes in Psalms, and the major techniques of rhyme, repetition, and free verse. What do you think?"

"It sounds great to me. In fact, I'd like to take notes myself."

I drank from my cup of tea. "I probably couldn't squeeze it into my schedule any other time, but it just so happens my kids are working on some research papers in the library most of next week. It would be ideal timing to do it Monday, Tuesday, or Wednesday while they're scheduled with someone else."

"Are you sure you want to go to all that trouble?" Jack said.

"I'd love to do it. Really I would."

"How about next Tuesday?" he asked.

"Tuesday it is," I returned and inwardly rejoiced. Even in a totally academic setting, it was an opportunity to share something positive about Scriptures to searching students. For this I was deeply grateful!

1:40 P.M. Faculty room.

The teacher's lounge was usually a loud and noisy place except for today: the few faculty members who shared the same planning period were detained in other parts of the building. Now peace and quiet reigned, and it was good. The calming atmosphere provided me with the time to reflect on the day's events and the temptation I'd had to stay home. True, I still felt drowsy and worn-out, but I could clearly see the purpose in my coming.

Just after I slipped off my shoes, leaned back and closed my eyes to rest, I was startled by a heavy rapping on the lounge door. Only students knocked like that.

"Coming!" I shouted and reached down for my shoes.

The banging persisted. "I said I was coming," I yelled a second time and began to hop on one foot while I maneuvered to put my shoe on the other. Bang! Bang! Bang! For a second I had the fleeting vision of a life-size Woody Woodpecker waiting for me on the opposite side of the door.

"Nancy! It's you," I said to the office girl and stepped into the hall.

"Miss Campbell, you got to come quick," she blurted out.

"What's wrong? Go where?" I inquired.

It's Henri. She's in the first floor rest room, crying her eyes out. She won't let anyone else help and she keeps asking for you."

"Do you know what it's about?"

"Henri's my best friend. She tells me everything except whatever's been bugging her this week. She got a note last period from Cliff, her boyfriend. I think that's what started it."

"I'll go on up. You make sure the office knows where she is."

"They already do. Mrs. Smith saw this was your planning time and she told me to go find you."

"I can't believe it," I said and shut the lounge door behind us.

"What do you mean?" Nancy asked.

I checked in my pants pocket for my keys and then rushed with Nancy to the nearby stairs. "There are so many ho-hum days when nothing out of the ordinary happens," I explained, "and then *poof*. There are some others when I feel more involved. Needed. You know."

We said little else as we made our way to the rest room. Once there, Nancy spoke, "I hope you can make her feel better, Miss Campbell."

"I'll do my best," I concluded. "And Nancy, could you tell Mrs. Smith I'll be right over as soon as we figure this one out? Try to keep kids from coming in until we're through, all right?"

She answered yes and darted across the hall.

It was a pathetic sight to discover Henrietta wedged into a far corner of the long narrow room. She was seated with her knees pulled up to her chest and her torso slumped forward. Quickly I stopped by a sink and moistened some paper towels, then sat down next to Henri on the cold hard floor and touched her arm. The sounds of her anguish diminished when she realized I had come.

"I heard you wanted to talk to me, Henrietta. How can I help?"

"I'm such a fool, Miss C. Such a stupid, worthless fool," she sobbed.

"Why do you say that? You were a little quiet in class today, but you seemed fine. Why all these tears?"

"I hate myself!"

"Henri, what happened? Tell me, please? I want to know."

She reached into her lap and produced the damp, crumpled letter. "Here," she cried, "maybe this will make you see what a fool I've been."

I flattened the letter on my knee with my opened palms. From what I could read, it was a farewell letter from Cliff. His words were shockingly graphic and totally uncomplimentary. I folded the note and tore it in half. "When he says good-bye, he really means good-bye," I commented.

"He called me some awful names. He said I was already used up. That I made him sick."

"What brought this on, Henri? Why the note?"

"Miss C., can't you guess?" she asked.

"I'd rather hear it from you."

She brushed her hair back and answered, "You'll hate me."

"No, I won't."

"You won't want me back at your fellowship group."

"You know I will," I said. "Try to tell me what this is all about, Henri. Please?"

"Last week. All he hammered on was touching and fooling around. Him to me. Me to him. He said if I didn't do something to prove I loved him . . . well . . . then I just didn't love him, that's all. Finally last night I said yes. All the way. I went along because I thought he'd want me more. He'd know I cared about him."

She took a deep breath and continued, "Now I'm a tramp and it'll be all over school. I thought it was what he wanted."

"Here," I interrupted. "Paper towels are all I have. Let's pretend they're Kleenex."

"It's all such a mess," Henrietta wept. "How can I ever face him again? And why does he think he's okay for pushing me to do it, and I'm all wrong for going along? My sister used to call it a second standard."

"I think she meant a double standard," I corrected.

"Yeah, that's it."

"That's a pretty common notion among a lot of people, especially in this particular area. What applies to males does not apply to females, and vice versa."

"I think it stinks. If it's right for one, it ought to be right for both," she said and swabbed her forehead with a wet towel.

"Or," I added, "if something's wrong for one, it's wrong for both?"

"Well, of course," she answered with total calmness.

"Henri, how are you going to handle this?"

"For starters, at least I don't have to worry about being pregnant. Cliff thought ahead on that one."

"And?"

She paused a minute and looked at me. "Do you think I'm a tramp?"

"No, Henrietta. I don't mean to minimize your situation or the consequences of what's happened. I think you've just fallen for one of the oldest lines in history: prove your love to me on my terms. Your body, Henri, *is your body*, not Cliff's or anyone else's to make demands on."

"I thought I'd lose him if I didn't go along. He even told me that. Now I see he got what he came for and it's time to split. He lays a guilt trip on me and he'll probably turn around to find some other girl to use. He told me I wasn't his first, you know."

We let a minute pass between us when neither of us spoke. Then I began, "Do you think you could have avoided this?"

"I sure could have. I'd rather have lost him some other way than this one. He wasn't worth it. *This* wasn't worth it."

"Henri, it's going to take you some time to put this all in perspective. It's important that you deal with it, though. I don't mean so much with Cliff, I mean with you inside." I pointed to my heart. "In here."

"I know," she answered. "I get what you mean."

"Henri, how do you feel now?"

"Pretty lousy. Tired. Confused. I'd like to get on my ten-speed and ride for miles and miles."

"Why don't you?"

"Maybe I will tonight," she stated. "And I'd like to think over what you said one time in that fellowship group at Lorrain's house."

"What was that?" I asked.

"Something about God's love even when we blow it. I . . . I don't believe like the rest of you, Miss C., but I'm going to give

it some thought. Maybe one day . . . well . . . you know."
"When you want to talk about it, I'd like to listen."
Henri cleared her throat and picked at some lint on her Levi's while I wound my watch. "Henri, the bell's going to ring soon and I've got to collect my things and get back upstairs for my last class. Are you going to be okay?"
"I guess so."
"Why don't you check with Mrs. Smith next door and see if you can stay with her the last forty-five minutes until school's out? Unless you want to go back to class?"
"No. My eyes are burning, and I bet I look a mess. I don't think I can take everyone staring at me. Tomorrow morning, maybe. Today, no."
"I think that's a wise choice," I replied and stood.
Henri continued to sit on the floor and she focused her attention on my outstretched hand. "Come on, Henri," I said. "Let me help lift you up."
She furrowed her eyebrows together. "But you already did, Miss C. You already did."

4:30 P.M. Bedroom.
More than anything I longed to go to sleep. I sat on the edge of the mattress debating whether to take an evening nap at that moment, or wait a few hours and retire early for the night. I kicked off my shoes and swung around to lay on the bedspread. With my hands as an additional cushion under my head, I contemplated my own exhaustion and the happenings of the past ten hours.
It was quite natural to relay my feelings in prayer. "Dear Father, it is Your precise timing which has made all this possible. First with Blythe this morning, then with Jack at lunch, and lastly with Henrietta. We both know I would have missed so much if I had stayed home. No teacher substitute could have taken my place. At least not today.
"God, thank You for using me these past hours in three separate and unique encounters. It makes me smile to see how You can order my steps even when I feel dazed and strained. I confess I don't always see You working in my life and I don't always feel necessary where I teach, but today will be forever special to me. Thanks for providing new open doors in my own

small world. Thanks for every new chance to reach where I am. I love you."

Although I intended to relax only a few moments and get up for a bite to eat, my fatigue got the better of me. In seconds I drifted off in sweet slumber. It was the deep, refreshing sleep of restoration. And like every other gift that day, it came directly from the Father's hand.

> *Do you not know? Have you not heard? The Everlasting God, the Lord, the creator of the ends of the earth does not become weary or tired. His understanding is inscrutable. He gives strength to the weary, and to him who lacks might He increases power. Though youths grow weary and tired, and vigorous young men stumble badly, yet those who wait for the Lord will gain new strength; they will mount up with wings like eagles, they will run and not get tired, they will walk and not become weary.*
>
> (Isaiah 40:28-31)

Father, you are my strength whether I'm awake or asleep. You are my God, my Lord, my Life. Amen.

13

Letters

Dear Betsy,

I wanted to wait a few days before I shared some reflections with you. I hope you're feeling more rested now than you were last week. Please know your family has been in my prayers since the moment I learned of your father's sudden death. The girls in our fellowship group want you to know they are praying, too.

You may not realize this, but I understand something of your loss because my own father died about seven years ago, coincidentally over Father's Day weekend. I'll never forget the overwhelming sensation at that time of numbness, confusion, disbelief, anger, and more.

Since then I've learned there are no pat answers to why life takes a sudden turn one way or another. I hope you have not been smothered by well-meaning Christian friends who try to explain away what has happened and what hurts deep inside.

The pain you feel is so intensely personal that no one can fathom its depth. The answers are likely so complex that no one can comprehend what might have caused or prevented this tragedy. Wrestle with these questions if you choose, Betsy, but you may do well to wait until you're stronger.

For several years before my own father's death my family had hints that his life was drawing to a close. Even so, this foreknowledge did not remove the sting or ease the ache. Death is always a hard one to handle, but as I look back tonight I can see there were some common remedies which gradually helped heal the loss. They were time, prayer, and getting together with a good, good listener.

You and I have had many talks. We have laughed until our sides ached, and we have both shared in earnest. You have always been open with me about your growing faith in our heavenly Father. And, quite simply, I'm convinced this will see you through.

Take care of yourself. You are special.

Teacher and friend,
Miss J. Campbell

Dear Andy,

How pleased I was to get your letter and learn you are spending your entire summer in the sunny state of California. As you might expect, we've had a solid week of rain, rain and more rain.

I'm fine. What a treat it is to sleep in until nine or ten o'clock if I want and then stay up late! By the way, I passed your hello on to Miss Nelson the last time we met for supper. She wants to know why *she* didn't get a Mickey Mouse souvenir from Disneyland like you sent me!

Andy, on a more serious note, I'm sorry to learn about your parents' divorce. In the history of the whole world I don't think there was ever a painless divorce. Not only for the separating adults, but especially for the children who may feel powerless and trapped in the middle of an awful situation.

There's no way I can begin to respond to all the questions and comments you posed in your letter, Andy. It's probably not much comfort, but divorce rates are very high these days and there are a lot of kids experiencing the same thing. *You aren't alone.* Many of your friends back at school are struggling to cope with their own feelings of brokenness just like you. Just like me when I was your age.

Can I share a dream of mine with you on this subject? I pray that eventually I'll have time to write a small book on what divorce does to children and young adults. Somehow it has a way of burning a kind of rejection and insecurity right into our human fabric. As you are discovering on your own, those scars can be quite deep. I know it's a hard statement to accept, Andy, but even today I still sometimes hurt because of what happened long ago in my life. And I think if more adults were honest, I believe they would admit the same thing too.

You wrote in your letter that you felt pretty worthless. That's not justified, Andy. You're one of the most creative students I've ever had. You are a fine young scholar, and you most certainly have the gift to excel in every sport you set your hand to. Last winter and spring proved that! How can you believe you have nothing to offer anymore?

This is short, but I've got to close. My cat and I are due at the vet's in about fifteen minutes. Before you ask, it's Tula who gets the checkup; I'm just going along for the ride! (Grin!)

You take care and keep up with your art, sports, and all those other talents. Don't get too much sun or you'll never be able to adjust to the drizzle back home!

Be good,
Miss J. Campbell

Dear Mr. & Mrs. Krahler,

My warmest greetings to both of you and your daughter. It's hard to believe Alicia is reading college catalogs. It seems like yesterday she sat in my classroom with bubble gum, braces, and long pigtails! Please give her my best and thank her for the note she inserted in your letter.

Despite this brief delay I trust my response arrives in time for you to present your request to your church board. In answer to your first question, yes, I sometimes speak on the topic "The Christian and the Occult." Like lots of teens I became intrigued with astrology when I was in high school. Keep in mind I wasn't a Christian then and was greatly influenced by a couple of close friends who dabbled in seances. I don't think I ever went totally overboard like some of them, but I confess I was genuinely fascinated by areas of the supernatural.

Alicia was also correct when she told you I met Jeane Dixon one-on-one during my senior year. I don't know if I can reconstruct our encounter to answer all your questions, but I'll try.

It all started when I heard Jeane was scheduled to speak for a few seminars in my city. I did a little investigative work to find out where she would be staying and what flight she would be on. Allowing so much time for her to get from the airport to her first stop, I planned to be at the hotel, blend in with other reporters and bring back the biggest scoop my high school newspaper had ever printed. I figured I'd be some kind of heroine because just about every kid I knew was interested in fortune telling. Who could dispute she wasn't the top person in her field?

I want you to know I'm not proud of this now, but I literally conned my way into going. Academically I was a good student and *this was kind of an educational experience for school*, so that was that.

When I pulled into the parking lot I was thrilled to see Jeane's limousine directly behind me. I flew into the hotel lobby and quickly sat behind my opened newspaper to watch and wait. What could be more dramatic? Once Jeane registered I got up and followed her to her room. It was when she dismissed the bellboy that I filled her doorway to introduce myself. Don't ask me why other reporters weren't there; all I knew was that I wasn't going to let this opportunity pass by.

Jeane invited me in. She scolded me for skipping my afternoon classes and then chatted about all sorts of things. I'd read one of her books the day before, so I was naturally full of questions. She showed *great* patience in answering each of them, and I found her very warm and friendly. Just before I was ready to leave she volunteered to read my fortune. I couldn't believe this was happening to me. While my friends were bored to death back in algebra class I was having my future read by one of the greats!

To be sure, I talked about that interview for days, and everything she said made terrific sense to me at the time. Yet as exciting as it was for me to meet Jeane then, I'd have a much different angle of questions and enthusiasm if I met with her now.

You were right when you wrote that kids can easily get entangled and preoccupied with the supernatural. Movies, television, books, and peer pressure bombard them with areas of the occult all the time. I've read of so many cases where teenagers got involved innocently (usually for fun) and were dragged over a period of time into utter darkness. That's why my presentation stresses three basic ideas: we need to know what occult activities are so we can deal intelligently with them; we must acknowledge they are not from God nor condoned by Him; and we need to be under God's special armor as outlined in Ephesians 6:10-18.

Enclosed you'll find a list of some books which you might like to purchase for your youth group in case we don't get together on a mutual date soon. It's important that kids get answers to questions when they are asking.

I look forward to hearing from you in the near future.

Cordially,
Jean Marie Campbell

Dear Mr. Lowell,

Many thanks for the special arrangements you made to fit *The Hiding Place* motion picture into your already overcrowded schedule.

I must say I was surprised a few months ago when a representative of World Wide Pictures told me I was the first public school teacher to ever request the film, but I was very disappointed to learn *The Hiding Place* was scheduled so far in advance I'd never be able to show it this year. After praying and waiting three months I decided to try World Wide Pictures again. This time I was referred to you, and you arranged for me to show the film. How I thank you.

The only way I could handle the film at school was from a purely academic point of view. I argued that if we show a presentation by the Jewish Theological Seminary at my grade level when we teach *The Diary of Anne Frank*, then why couldn't we expose our students to another side of the same issue if a different film were available? Especially if I were paying the royalty fee myself to keep from using school funds? The film has great historical significance! It could only enrich our studies!

I want you to know I didn't receive a single complaint from any student, parent, or teacher after showing the film. Of course, I could never discuss the spiritual influence of the story with my students. But then why should I have to? The ten Booms' faith in God speaks so well for itself.

You might be interested to learn I asked my students to write a brief summary on the film's effectiveness and to include whether the movie would be beneficial for next year's classes. I received many impressive observations, and my students gave an overwhelming yes for its future use *anywhere*.

I see no reason why other public schools could not benefit from the film, providing teachers stay strictly within the purpose of their curriculum guidelines. I urge you to seriously consider this kind of ministry as you plan future showings of *The Hiding Place*. It is a most remarkable film.

Thanks for your help in making this dream come true.

Sincerely,
Jean Marie Campbell

Dear Heavenly Father,

It's 1:00 in the morning and I can't sleep. All I do is think and thrash about restlessly.

There are times like tonight when I wish I could retreat from my friends, from my classroom, from everyone. There are times when successful and rewarding moments are actually months apart. Sometimes I'm bored with the monotonous routine of getting up and going to school to face some students who care, and others who hate me and all that I stand for.

I don't mean to overindulge in self-pity, it's just I so often get discouraged and crushed with my own smallness. Is all this really worth it? Is it that I expect too much or too little? Do I try too hard or not enough? Have I brought You honor and has my motivation been pure? I don't know, Father, I don't know the answers anymore.

Today, among other things, Tim called me a freaky religious snob when I sent him out for spitting in Barb's face. I know he was upset and screamed insults to everyone nearby, but is that how I portray you? Is that how I come across? A kind of self-righteous snob?

Did You ever feel like quitting, Jesus? Did You ever get tired of trying? Of crying inside? Did You wonder if anyone really understood? No matter how much I stumble, it is You I *want* to please. But is that enough, Lord Jesus? Is that enough for a king?

Quiet me, Lord. From time to time remind me I'm no miracle worker. The truth is, I don't have to do it all. The truth is, I *can't*. Just help me through these uneventful days which blend one with another. Please make me into the productive soil that yields faithfulness in all circumstances. Exciting days as well as the more often mundane.

In all this draw me close to You.

I . . . I love You.

Jean

14

Join Us

"Let the congregation rise for the benediction," the minister spoke in his strong, clear voice. "And let us hear these final words from Jude: 'Now to Him who is able to keep you from stumbling, and to make you stand in the presence of His glory blameless with great joy, to the only God our Savior, through Jesus Christ our Lord, be glory, majesty, dominion and authority, before all time and now and forever.' Amen and amen."

The organ burst forth with praise as the minister made his way to a rear sanctuary door. Lines of people were already forming to shake his hand and offer greetings after his Sunday morning message. Anticipating my own quick departure, I sat back down on the pew to gather my purse and Bible and to put the church hymnal inside its rack.

"Don't you know church is over?" came the question behind me.

"Max!" I exclaimed and jumped up to shake his hand. "I can't believe my eyes! How many years has it been?"

"At least eight, I'd say. Last time I saw you was at our high-school graduation. It's good to see you!"

"You don't look like you've aged a day, Max. You even part your platinum blond hair on the same side. Dare I still call you Goldilocks?"

He chuckled and let go of my hand. "You remember my old nickname?"

"How could I forget?" I returned. "Max, do you have a minute? Can you sit down and tell me what you've been doing? It's been about five or six years since either of us wrote."

Max edged his way from the pew behind to join me in mine. As soon as he sat down he glanced at my wrist. "That watch," he groaned. "You still wear that watch? Oh, Jean!"

"Oh, Max!" I echoed back. "I know you're only jealous. I can tell a true Mickey Mouse fan when I see one, and deep down inside I've always sensed you were a faithful follower."

"Well, maybe a little bit," he admitted. "Mickey was my idol at one time."

I smiled. "That's better, Max."

He punched my arm and laughed, "Back when I was four years old! Ha!"

"Oh, Max, enough of this," I said and waved my hands in a sign of truce. "Tell me, how long have you gone to this church? I woke up this morning and decided today was the day to drive over here and visit. A friend recommended I hear their new minister."

Max's face brightened. "What a coincidence. We don't go here, either. My wife and I are heading back home today after a week with her relatives. By the way, I want you to meet Betty. She's downstairs with her sister."

I grinned in surprise. "I had no idea you got married."

"Yeah. Right after college," he explained. "Then I taught a couple years at a Christian high school, and now I'm assistant headmaster there. How's that for promotion?"

"I'm glad for you," I replied. "Congratulations."

"The school's about two hundred miles east of here, just over the state border. Betty teaches there also. We really believe, Jean, the Christian private schools are the coming thing. I, for one, will be glad to see that day arrive," he said with authority.

"You have an interesting point of view," I stated. "But both you and I came up through the ranks of public education, and we seem to have done pretty well. Haven't we?"

"Perhaps you've got me there," he agreed. "That reminds me. Weren't you considering a career in teaching? I remember something about that in a few of your old letters. Did you ever follow through?"

"Oh, yes," I noted. "I got my degree in English and secondary education. I've done a little writing and speaking on the side over the years since graduation, but nearly all of my time has been absorbed in teaching."

Max pulled out a pack of cherry *Lifesavers* and tore the bright paper wrapper. "Want one?" he asked, put a piece in his mouth, and offered the candy roll. I accepted and thanked him. Max groped for his pocket and continued, "So, are you in the public or private scene?"

"Public," I answered, "and I enjoy it."

"But how? How can you stand it there, Jean? The drugs. Violence. Worldly values. From what I read, every year it gets worse and worse to manage kids and survive."

"I don't pretend to love all aspects of what I do, especially utilizing so much time in discipline," I responded. "But it's certainly not a waste of my time, Max. *No way.*"

I could tell by his expression that an idea had sparked in his mind. "Listen, Jean, we can always use good English teachers back at my school. I already know of one and possibly two openings for this fall. Why don't you come and join us? I'm serious now. What do you say? It'd be like old times again, only better. And you wouldn't have to fight for your life like you do out in *the jungle!*" He hissed and brought his hand up to mimic a ferocious lion. "Think of it. No more headaches! No more hassles!"

"Max, I don't think you understand," I said in earnest. "There's a lot of work to be done where I am. The public schools aren't hopeless, *but if you keep pulling out all our committed teachers and students, it just may end up that way.*"

"Uh-oh," he confessed. "I think I've touched a sensitive nerve."

"I'm not an enemy of the Christian schools, Max. I'm just deeply concerned over the dire need we have for Christian examples out in the mainstream. In all levels. Among students. Faculty. Administrators. Board members. Max, how can we reach people in that particular world if we're not in it?"

"You have a point, Jean," he replied seriously. "But a lot of people I know have given up on the public schools. A lot of them are teaching right now in my own system. They're tired. They say it's too much of a strain in public education anymore. They say they're too restricted in what they can do, say, enforce, teach. *They say the system is much too big and complex these days for one person to make a difference. So why not go where they can?*"

"Max, Max," I sighed and stopped to think. It surprised us both when I found my throat constricting and my eyes watery. "A long time ago," I continued, "I heard a theologian say, 'It is better to light one candle than to curse the darkness.' I like that saying and I think of it every time I toy with the idea of leaving public education for another life. Maybe your friends and I have a different approach with our kids, Max, I don't know. But I sincerely believe I'm one candle and I *can* make a difference."

"Jean, I get your point," Max responded, "but lights are lights wherever they go. My friends did not stop being lights when they came to my school. Christian institutions have a ministry and a place in our world, too."

"Forgive me, Max. I know what you say is true. I guess because I have such a burden for where I am, I'd like to recruit all the committed people I can find. My first instinct is to want to channel your friends right back out into the mainstream, headaches and all. Why? Maybe it's because I see the cross section and larger numbers of people who are reachable within the public setting. Maybe it's because I believe a lot of these people are hurting. Maybe it's because I hurt with them."

"It sounds to me like you've found a special gift that works for you. Level with me, Jean. Is there a secret you've discovered along the way?"

I glanced at the empty pews around us while I considered his question. For the first time I realized we were the only ones left in the large sanctuary. "I don't know if I've ever considered it a secret," I admitted. "I teach. I discipline. I listen. I respond. Almost daily I remind myself that all of my kids have worth and dignity in our Father's eyes, and I pray for the competence to treat them accordingly. I know it's a pretty simple philosophy, Max, but that's what mine boils down to.

"Think back for a moment to all the teachers you and I had. The ones we loved the most were touchable, flesh-and-blood persons who cared about us individually. We practically broke our backs to cooperate with them and produce quality work. On the other hand, the instructors we disliked were mechanical, distant, and preoccupied with their own importance, never ours. Most of us dragged our feet for them and hated every minute of their classes. If you and I could spot our teachers' motivation years ago, how much more do our own kids see right through us?

"When all is said and done, I think what makes the difference, and what we'll be remembered for is whether we've cared. I don't think it's in our hairstyles, or clothes, or class assignments, or rules, or even what we taught that will necessarily leave the lasting impression with our students. These things carry importance, of course, but in the long run I think our paramount success will be measured by our ability to accept our students where they are, to encourage them, and to care."

I stopped when I saw a growing smile spread across Max's face. "All right, Max. What did I say now?"

"Oh," he answered, "it's good to hear someone talk like that. You've grown a lot, Jean. The schools, all of them, need teachers like you. Not everyone has your commitment to make a difference."

"One of these years I just may take you up on your offer to come over and teach at a Christian school. But I don't imagine it will be anytime soon. And who knows? Perhaps one day the urge will hit you to devote your skills and concerns to public education. There's a need, Max, such a gigantic need for more candles out there."

"I believe you, Jean, and I'll think it over. Remember," he said and raised his index finger, "it is better to light one candle than to curse the darkness!"

I pulled my hand from my skirt pocket and lifted a finger likewise. "Right, Max," I concluded. "You're absolutely right."

Father, here am I. Use me in Your world. Choose me for Your service. Amen.

Launching

i am Your servant
Father
and i am waiting
for even Your tiniest of signals
that i may soar and wing
into the broadening skies of Your labor.
at Your call let me sail
unencumbered
arms wide
on the upward winds of tomorrow
to rise in fuller, richer service.
please oh please
navigate my course.
help me mount
higher, straighter
by the sweet rush of Your Spirit
to purposes and worlds i have never reached.
is it time now?
You know
i am Your servant
Father
and i am coming.
i am coming.
i am coming.
amen.